MANY THINGS IN PARABLES

Jesus and His Modern Critics

Charles W. Hedrick

Westminster John Kn
LOUISVILLE • LOND

Book design by Sharon Adams
Cover design by Pam Poll Graphic Design
Cover art: The Good Shepherd *(oil on canvas), by Philippe de Champaigne (1602-74). Courtesy of Giraudon / Bridgeman Art Library.*

First edition
Published by Westminster John Knox Press
Louisville, Kentucky

This book is printed on acid-free paper that meets the American National Standards Institute Z39.48 standard. ♾

PRINTED IN THE UNITED STATES OF AMERICA

04 05 06 07 08 09 10 11 12 13 — 10 9 8 7 6 5 4 3 2 1

Library of Congress Cataloging-in-Publication Data

Hedrick, Charles W.
Many things in parables : Jesus and his modern critics / Charles W. Hedrick.—1st ed.
p. cm.
Includes bibliographical references and index.
ISBN 0-664-22427-X (alk. paper)
1. Jesus Christ—Parables. I. Title.

BT375.3.H44 2004

2003064519

For the curious stud
Who finds questi
More interes
Than grand so
A true pe
Of great value.

Contents

Preface

Matthew, Mark, and Luke (the Synoptic Gospels) portray Jesus as an apocalyptic figure who announced the end of the world and the imminent arrival of God's reign (for example, Mark 1:14 and 13:24–37). They also portray him as a teacher of religious wisdom embodying the highest ethical sensitivities of the Hebrew prophets, an ethic that stressed life in the world (for example, Mark 12:28–32; Matt 5:44; 9:13; 23:23). On the other hand, John's Gospel portrays him as a revealer of divine wisdom and knowledge (for example, 8:21–30; 12:44–50). None of the gospels portray him as a traditionalist, but rather as a harsh critic of the temple cult (for example, Mark 11:15–18) and Pharisaic legalism (for example, Matt 23:13–39).

Not every saying preserved as a part of Jesus' public discourse fits comfortably into these categories, however. For example, Matt 10:16 (= *Thom* 39.3) is a rather astonishing saying, when considered apart from its literary context. Matthew includes the saying in Jesus' instructions to his disciples preceding a preaching mission (Matt 10:1–11:1; note that 10:1–6 and 11:1 are literary frames for the speech). Readers are influenced by the literary context ("I send you out as sheep in the midst of wolves") and miss the shock of the saying. In such a social context the sheep are always at risk and must be shrewd (that is, they must be "sly like snakes") and ever careful to guard their integrity (that is, be "guileless as doves"). Were it otherwise, how could they become "lights to the world" and "salt for the earth" (Matt 5:13–16)?

In *Thomas*, on the other hand, the saying is contrasted with the actions of the Pharisees and scribes. Although they possessed the keys of knowledge, the Pharisees and scribes deliberately hindered people from finding knowledge.

In this context, the saying urges a reader to acquire wisdom and renounce duplicity, as the Pharisees and scribes had failed to do (see Matt 23:1–2). The two literary contexts where the saying is met in the gospels mask its subversive character, for each provides the saying with a context that makes a reasonable understanding possible.

The saying was originally independent of these literary contexts, however, and when the saying is removed from the context, it comes with a certain shock: "You must be sly as snakes and simple as pigeons." In Mediterranean antiquity the snake was thought to be a sly, crafty, duplicitous, and deceptive creature. The word translated "sly" connotes "sensible" or "prudent," but linked with the snake it takes on a sharply negative tone—at once guileful and malicious. The snake, after all, deceived Eve (Gen 3:1, 13), and as Paul later noted, the snake did it by villainy or cunning (2 Cor 11:3). Hence the translation "sly" or "crafty" is more appropriate than "wise" or "prudent."

The second half of the saying makes a surprising contrast with the first: "Be simple as pigeons." Doves and pigeons belong to the same family (*columbidae*), and hence are similar. They are distinguished, however, in Leviticus, where the poor are instructed to bring for sacrifice either "turtledoves" or "young pigeons" (Lev 1:14). Different Hebrew words are used for each bird. The Septuagint (the ancient Greek translation of the Hebrew Bible) translates the Hebrew for "pigeons" with the same Greek word used in Matt 10:16. This same word is also found in Luke 2:24, where it is translated "pigeon." In English the word "pigeon" has a strong negative connotation when used figuratively. A "pigeon" is a target in a confidence scam. "Pigeons" are simple, naive, or innocent people, easily swindled by crafty con artists. Some of this same negative character attached itself to the word "pigeon" in Mediterranean antiquity. In the Hebrew Bible, for example, Ephraim (a poetic way of referring to the northern nation of Israel in the period of the Divided Kingdoms) is figuratively described as a "simple pigeon" (that is, without understanding, Hos 7:11). The gentle character and guilelessness of pigeons was proverbial in Mediterranean antiquity. In the second half of Matt 10:16 Jesus urges readers to be simple like pigeons. "Simple" in the context of the first half of the saying carries the idea of guilelessness and innocent harmlessness as opposed to guile, deceit, or cunning. "Be sly as snakes and simple as pigeons" is therefore a paradox—an oxymoron, and hence it is self-contradictory. Each half of the saying contradicts the other. If you are shrewd and cunning, you are not naive and simple.

Paul uses similar language in Rom 16:19. "Be wise . . . and guileless . . . ," he instructs his reader. Yet Paul, like Matthew and Thomas, qualifies the saying so that his meaning is clear: "Be learned in the good and pure as regards evil." Paul's saying is no paradox, but simply moral exhortation where the meaning is clear because it has a context. Jesus' saying, however, lacks an application or a context, and leaves a reader groping for some way to relate it to life: "Be as crafty as a con man and as vulnerable as his pigeon."

The saying ridicules community wisdom by contrasting different character traits valued in community: shrewdness and prudence, candor and purity. But when associated with snakes and pigeons, and counterpoised, community morals are caricatured and turned on their ear. Shrewdness can be deceitful and purity can translate into gullibility. In any case readers cannot be both at the same time even if they wanted. Like certain other sayings of Jesus, this oxymoron perplexes and teases but offers no clue how to apply it to life.

Such teasing language suits neither the apocalyptic prophet's sense of urgency in the face of cosmic catastrophe, nor the serious moral instructions of a religious teacher, and it is in strong contrast to the direct authoritative voice of a divine revealer. On the other hand, the saying does fit with the parables in both spirit and vision, for Jesus' parabolic discourse is also inconsistent with the categories apocalyptic prophet, religious teacher, and divine revealer. In order to fit the parables into these categories modern critics are forced to use a variety of strategies whereby secular stories are transformed into apocalyptic warnings, moral instruction, and divine revelations.

On their surface the parables are secular stories about common life in first-century Palestine. They do not moralize, nor does the narrative voice of the parables condemn or commend the behavior of characters in the stories. The stories reflect neither apocalyptic despair nor imminent cosmic destruction. They are patently a-religious—neither advocating nor critiquing any particular view. The narrator of the parables has no opinions, is completely self-effacing, and is silent on matters of faith, morals, and religion. For example, the Pharisee and the Toll Collector (Luke 18:9–13) present two clearly contradictory courses of life in Palestinian Judaism—but the narrator neither takes sides nor criticizes.

Such moral ambiguity, a distinguishing feature of Jesus' stories, situates the parables in some respects with what the literary critic Northrop Frye calls the ironic mode, a style characterized by "complete objectivity and suppression of all explicit moral judgments."[1] For Frye, the ironic mode reflects the attitude of a poet who produces "a dispassionate construction of a literary form, with all assertive elements, implied or expressed, lacking. Irony, as a mode, is born from the low mimetic; it takes life exactly as it finds it, but the ironist fables without moralizing and has no object but his subject."[2] Fabling without moralizing, as Frye puts it, is precisely what the narrative voice of the parables does, as this book hopes to show.

This book is written for an average reader. It aims at summarizing the current state of parables study, at unmasking the assumptions driving the strategies by which scholars read the parables, and at clarifying a reasonable, if modest, comprehensive theory for how parables work. My hope is that these chapters will enable average readers to engage the parables for themselves as first-century fictions.

As is always the case, no book is completely the work of a single individual. Every writer draws on the ideas of others. In the following pages readers will note how much I have learned from other scholars, particularly those scholars whose work has ensured them a permanent place in the history of parables study: Adolf Jülicher, Charles H. Dodd, Joachim Jeremias, Amos N. Wilder, Norman Perrin, Robert W. Funk, Dan Otto Via Jr., and John Dominic Crossan. Others have contributed much, but these scholars have provided the landmark studies, which represent the point of departure for any serious study of the parables.

I am grateful to Southwest Missouri State University for a brief sabbatical leave in the fall semester of 2002 to complete the writing of this book, and to my colleagues, Charles W. Hedrick Jr. and James R. Hubbart, for critiquing certain translations.

Charles W. Hedrick
Christmas 2003

Introduction

WHAT'S THE SITUATION? AN EMBARRASSING STATE OF AFFAIRS

Shortly before the death (4 B.C.E.) of Herod the Great, king of Judea, Jesus was born. According to early Christian tradition, his birth took place at Bethlehem (Matt 2; Luke 2), a few miles south of Jerusalem. He was reared, however, in the Galilee region at Nazareth, a tiny village in the hills a short distance from Sepphoris, where for most of Jesus' life Herod Antipas directed the affairs of his tetrarchy (Galilee and Perea). Virtually everything known about Jesus' public life comes from the early Christian Gospels of Matthew, Mark, and Luke, written decades after his death. Nothing is known of his private life. The gospels describe a number of Jesus' public acts and preserve sayings and stories attributed to him in the course of his public career in the first third of the first century. Detailed reports exist of his death at the hands of the Romans during the prefecture of Pontius Pilate (26–36 C.E.).

The most prominent feature of Jesus' public discourse, to judge from the gospels, is the brief story form he popularized in his short career. These stories, dubbed *parables* since the latter part of the first century, on their surface are simply secular stories about aspects of village life in what the Romans knew as Syria-Palestine, and later simply as Judea. Through the years it has been easier to reconcile the gospel accounts of Jesus' *activities* with who Jesus is in the faith of the church than it has been to reconcile his *stories*, which on the surface are not religious at all. Since the first century, his stories have remained a conundrum for the New Testament critic. How is it possible, for example, to find something religiously significant about God—or human life, for that matter—from a very brief narrative about some woman putting yeast into a rather large measure of flour (Matt 13:33b; Luke 13:20b–21; *Thom* 96:1)? That issue—how to go from first-century secular story to "appropriate" religious explanation—has continued to be the fuse driving the fascination of the critic with Jesus' stories. In the hands of his critics, those who ponder and analyze his stories for their "true" meanings, Jesus has become many different people and his stories have been found to say many different things. All such critics claim their analyses open up the stories, giving expression to their true voice—and that claim creates the embarrassing situation in which the study of parables finds itself today.

THE CURRENT SITUATION

All biblical scholars want their colleagues and the reading public in general to regard their work as "scientific." Interpretation of literary texts of any sort, however, is different from the physical sciences. Perhaps the practice of New Testament studies is better regarded as an art form. It certainly seems to have more in common with the artist's easel than the chemist's test tubes. New Testament scholarship, like the physical sciences, proceeds on the basis of certain commonly held assumptions and generally agreed-on analytical techniques and methods. A glance at any competent introduction to the literature of the New Testament will confirm this statement. At a minimum, New Testament scholars must be thoroughly familiar with the languages and social history of the first-century world, as well as the history of prior scholarship on the New Testament. Even allowing for some flexibility in assumptions, methods, and familiarity with the vast body of knowledge undergirding New Testament studies, study of the parables, to judge from the results, seems more heavily indebted to opportunism and entrepreneurship than science. Few controls exist to limit the number of interpretations to the same parable. Each new book on the parables offers interpretations so divergent and contradictory from what preceded it as to distinguish the enterprise sharply from the physical sciences, which require that experiments be repeatable under the same conditions in order to be regarded as successful.

What differentiates the physical sciences from the study of parables is precisely the conditions under which the study is conducted. Parable scholars do not share a common set of assumptions about parables or follow the same techniques in explaining parables. They do not even agree on what a parable is, and consequently they do not agree on how parables function. In modern study of the parables, for example, a single parable is understood to reference the kingdom (i.e., rule) of God, illustrate a general (Christian) moral, reflect authentic and inauthentic existence, typify the exploitation of a peasant class, teach proper Christian behavior, reveal the mysteries of the end of the world, teach aspects of Christian theology, and much more.

Modern studies are continually able to dig out new treasures from these old parabolic fields. For example, according to W. O. E. Oesterley, the parable of a Fig Tree in a Vineyard (Luke 13:6–9) is "intended" to teach a specific summary truth, which is either: (1) life should be upright, moral, and provide evidence of good living; or (2) God is patient, giving even the evil person a chance to repent—but in its context in Luke, Oesterley avers, the parable teaches the need for repentance.[1] For Madeleine Boucher, this parable is Jesus' allegory on a particular situation in his public career. Individual elements in the narrative have a one-to-one relationship to religious values outside the narrative; for example, the owner of the fig tree represents God, the fig tree is Israel, and the fruit the tree fails to bear is justice and righteousness. Thus, according to Boucher, Jesus is telling Israel, in spite of its unfaithfulness, that it will be given a chance to repent and mend its ways.[2] For Peter Rhea Jones, the parable prophetically calls Israel to national repentance before God's patience is exhausted.[3] David Wenham finds three possible explanations for the parable: (1) It could be a Christian message that warns of the danger of deceiving yourself into thinking you are truly Christian if your life does not measure up to your confession; (2) it could be a first-century message to individual Jews that God's judgment will come upon you if you fail to repent; or (3) it could be Jesus' own message to the people of Israel that here is one last opportunity to repent.[4] Bernard Brandon Scott takes the parable as an image directly referencing the rule of God.[5]

In these few examples, the parable is taken to function as an allegory, an image, and a didactic narrative teaching moral lessons. It is "about" the kingdom of God, repentance, the national repentance of Israel, God's patience, the danger of self-deception, and the necessity of moral living. Thus this parable, in twentieth-century scholarship, teaches, references, and conceals many specific religious truths, both Jewish and Christian.

Clearly Jesus could not consciously have intended so many different things with his one parable. The very diversity and competitiveness of these interpretations renders them all suspect, particularly since each interpreter claims to have rendered the one proper meaning of the parable—to the exclusion of all others. This exclusiveness, associated with each interpretation, opens parable scholarship to the charge of opportunism and entrepreneurship. In the absence of any firm controls, parables apparently mean whatever interpreters can convince others they mean. An objective disinterested reader of these interpretations will likely conclude that parables, whatever they are and however they work, at the very least are capable of multiple readings, and would then be interested in the assumptions that enabled the different readings.

AN OUTLINE OF THE HISTORY OF SCHOLARSHIP ON THE PARABLES

Since the time of Jesus, the history of parables study has been marked by six major shifts in understanding parables. How Jesus used them cannot today be documented with any degree of confidence. We have no literary sources for the parables covering the period from Jesus to the Gospel of Mark (30 to 70 C.E.). The most we can say is those who heard Jesus tell them repeated them to others, making changes as appropriate to facilitate the narrator's understanding in the new performance. In that forty-or-so-year period before Mark wrote his gospel, the parables received a variety of explanations, some of which are thought to be preserved as interpretations to certain parables in the Synoptic Gospels.

We do know, however, how the parables were understood shortly after the middle of the first century. Mark is the earliest extant writer to report and explain the parables. From the time of Mark (ca. 70 C.E.) until the end of the nineteenth century, explanations of parables followed Mark's theory of what the parables were—allegorical narratives. The stories, rather simple on their surface, were thought to conceal many different things of importance pertaining to Christian faith, morals, instruction, values, and theology. The many, more or less common, things in the parables were treated as merely surface ciphers for concealed Christian religious truths. This way of reading parables has lasted for almost two thousand years and is still practiced today.

A truly modern study of the parables did not begin until the end of the nineteenth century with a German scholar, Adolf Jülicher, and his predecessor, A. B. Bruce.[6] Jülicher rejected the allegorical method; parables were simply not allegories, he argued. The many things in the parable flowed together to form a single image of two parts: a picture part (the parabolic story) and a substance part (the central idea of the story). The parable imaged a single moral concept; this single idea is what the parable was really about. While Jülicher's work had a great influence on subsequent study of the parables, it has never completely replaced allegorical interpretation, even in critical scholarship.

In 1935, a new understanding of parables emerged. C. H. Dodd, a British scholar, argued that parables were brief metaphors that referenced the kingdom of God. A metaphor is an image that talks about one thing under the guise of describing something else. By means of his parables, Jesus described the kingdom of God under the guise of aspects of common life in first-century

Palestine. At its simplest the parable is a metaphor or simile drawn from nature or common life, arresting the hearer by its vividness or strangeness, and leaving the mind in sufficient doubt about its precise application, thereby teasing it into active thought.[7]

Shortly after the beginning of the twentieth century, readers could choose between three rather different ways of reading parables: They were either allegories concealing many Christian truths, or illustrations of general moral truths, or metaphors that described the kingdom of God by means of common stories about life and nature. But few considered that any one of these strategies excluded the other two. Some scholars, lacking a consistent theory of parables, even applied all three strategies to different parables in the same study.

In 1967, Dan Otto Via Jr. proposed a completely different approach.[8] For Via, parables were literary creations that could be studied for their understanding of human existence as any appropriate literary text could be studied. He concluded that the parables were nonreferential "aesthetic objects," which could be studied like any artistic literature or like an object of art, such as painting and sculpture. In other words, the parables as narratives were important for their literary value, rather than for what Jesus may have intended to do with them.

In 1994, following Via's insights, I argued that parables were nonreferential "poetic fictions" that reflected the social world of first-century Palestinian Judaism.[9] A first-century audience would have engaged them as they did any story. In order to understand them as first-century stories, the parables must be read in the context of the values and culture of the first century. The parabolic stories of Jesus competed in the Palestinian marketplace with the ideological constructs used by Jewish auditors to make sense of their lives, by affirming or subverting their constructs and offering new opportunities for viewing life differently.

Simultaneously in 1994, William R. Herzog argued that parables were not referential but rather didactic stories. These narratives, according to Herzog, explore how human beings in the first century could break "the spiral of violence and cycle of poverty" created by a first-century elite class. They typify the oppression under which first-century peasants lived. Parables are not about theology but rather about "the gory details of how oppression served the interests of a ruling class." They do not describe God's intervention in human affairs but are designed to lead first-century human beings to change the oppressive conditions under which they lived. Thus, the parables are a kind of social analysis of the economic tyranny of first-century life.[10] In Herzog's view, Jesus was the leader of a peasant revolt, and his parables are about the sad circumstance of economic oppression in the first century.

AN ASIDE TO THE READER

This book aims at demystifying the parables by going behind such different conclusions to examine and evaluate methods and assumptions permitting these diverse explanations. Assumptions are like elevation and windage settings on the sights of a rifle. Elevation and windage settings determine the trajectory of the projectile. In short, assumptions control interpretations, just as elevation and windage determine projectile trajectory. For the most part, these assumptions are well known to scholars but not so well known to the general reader. For example, one major assumption concerns the literary context of the parables. Do introductions and conclusions to parables and the parables' larger narrative contexts in the gospels preserve authentic memory from the time of Jesus? This is a crucial issue that every reader of parables must answer. It cannot be avoided. As might be expected, scholars answer the question differently.

What is at issue, at least initially, is where does the reading of a parable begin—with the parable itself, with the literary context in which it appears, or with the scholars' interpretation of parables? The answer, of course, is contingent on the reader's interest. If one is interested in the evangelist's understanding of the parable, reading begins with the literary context, but if one is interested in the parable in the context of Jesus' public career some forty years or so earlier than the gospels, reading begins with the parable and ignores the literary setting. Those who begin with the literary setting proceed on the assumption that the *literary* context of the parable in the gospels (usually dated around and after 70 C.E.) accurately reflects the *social* context in the public career of Jesus (around 30 C.E.). Joachim Jeremias, for example, thought that virtually all the literary settings of the parables derived from the gospel writers but that a very few do preserve historical memory from the circumstances of Jesus' public career.[11] The rationale leading to such a conclusion should not be assumed, however, but shown by critical argument in every case—for it is equally possible (according to many, it is probable) that the literary settings constitute the evangelist's interpretation of the parable in the latter half of the first century. Studying the parable first, before considering its literary context, restores a logical historical sequence to the study of the parable. Jesus' invention of the parable in the social context of first-century life preceded the writing of the gospels. Literary contexts and interpretations in the gospels, whether from Jesus or not, of necessity must be a later reflection on the parables.[12]

PART 1

Theory

1

What Is a Parable?

The Evidence from the Gospels

Even the most biblically challenged reader, if asked "What is a parable?" would likely say, "Why, one of the stories Jesus told, of course"—such as the vicissitudes of a first-century farmer (the Sower, Mark 4:3–8), or the story about a dysfunctional family (the Prodigal Son, Luke 15:11–32). General agreement exists on this point among modern scholars, as well. In fact, virtually everyone thinks Jesus' stories constitute his characteristic form of discourse. A glance at any book devoted to parables will show this to be true. Unfortunately, such agreement does not resolve the issue, because early Christian literature does not restrict the term "parable" exclusively to narratives or stories, but uses it for a variety of other literary forms as well. This chapter will survey the use of the word "parable" in early Christian literature and assess what the diversity of forms means for the modern study of Jesus' parables.

PARABLES IN THE SYNOPTIC GOSPELS

We begin with the Synoptic Gospels, since these texts preserve most of the stories Jesus told and are among the earliest extant Christian writings. The Synoptic Gospels do not agree on what a parable is and, consequently, describe different literary forms as parables.[1] The word "parable" (*parabole*) is simply a transliteration of the Greek word used by the gospel writers. It means something cast (*bole*) alongside (*para*) something else. Hence, when the evangelists apply this term to the sayings of Jesus they are attributing a figurative character to them: parables say one thing but really mean something entirely different. By calling them "parable," the gospel writer is alerting the reader to that fact: "Be careful! Don't be misled by what it says. Look below the surface of this saying." In Matthew, Mark, and Luke, we find the following literary forms labeled parables: *narratives*, such as the story of the Samaritan (Luke 10:30–35); *proverbs*, such as the saying about the physician (Luke 4:23); *aphorisms;* and *images*, such as the verbal figure of the fig tree (Mark 13:28).

Even *straightforward discourse* is called "parable" in the gospels, although it has no obvious figurative significance—for example, Jesus' teaching on proper dining etiquette (Luke 14:8–10), or Jesus' rather unambiguous saying on defilement (Mark 7:14–17).

The synoptic evangelists apply "parable" to several different literary forms, thereby demonstrating they did not regard the term as designating a formal literary type. Rather, for the gospel writers a parable appears to be (1) any mode of Jesus' discourse whose simple or self-evident meaning is inconsistent with their understanding of Jesus' character and mission, or (2) any saying of Jesus so apparently banal that it could not possibly mean what it evidently says. Thus, the term "parable" functions for the synoptic evangelists as a hermeneutical tool, allowing them to achieve satisfactory religious meanings for difficult, obscure, or what they consider inappropriate sayings of Jesus. In modern scholarship the term "parable" is used regularly ambiguously. If we follow the lead of the early Christian gospels, the term should be regarded as a general designation to accommodate a variety of discourse.

A *narrative* is a literary form that tells a story (i.e., has a plot with characters and action), comprised, at a minimum, of a beginning, middle, and end. For example, the three parts of the parable of the Sower are Mark 4:3 (beginning), Mark 4:4–7 (middle), and Mark 4:8 (end).

A *proverb* is a short, pithy saying that summarizes some aspect of traditional community wisdom. It brings to language what is instantly clear and recognized as true, right, and proper by those who share in the life of the community. Frequently readers confuse proverbs and aphorisms, because these sayings share a similar tight form and pithy character.

An *aphorism* is a terse statement of a principle or precept usually unclear on its surface; the auditor/reader must ponder what is really at issue in the saying. The aphorism parades itself as a proverb but tends to undermine accepted community wisdom. Frequently the saying has a paradoxical character; for example, "Let the dead bury their own dead" (Luke 9:60); "A blind man is not able to lead a blind man, is he?" (Luke 6:39); or "be as shrewd as snakes and gullible as pigeons" (Matt 10:16).[2]

An *image* (or *figure*) is simply a picture with words representing a particular sensual experience expressed in language. It has no significance beyond what it is, but is used to intensify the reader's "visual" experience in the act of reading.[3]

PARABLES IN NONCANONICAL GOSPELS

Early Christian literature is far more extensive than just those texts in the New Testament. For example, eight complete early Christian gospels from the early centuries of the Christian era still exist today. In addition, fragments of seven other gospels have survived the ravages of time. Four other gospels are known from selected quotations in the works of other writers. Scholars have argued for the existence of still two others, earlier than the canonical gospels, preserved as sources used by the canonical authors, and we know of the existence of at least thirteen others by name. This makes a total of at least thirty-four gospels circulating in the early Christian period.[4] Only two of these noncanonical texts are known to preserve parables of Jesus, however: the *Gospel of Thomas* and the *Secret Book of James.*

Parables in *Thomas*

Thomas does not use the word "parable" but does have some of the characteristic narratives, or stories, designated as parable in the Synoptic Gospels (sayings 8, 9, 20, 21, 57, 63, 64, 65, 76, 96, 97, 98, 107, 109). Three of these are new parables, unknown prior to the discovery of a complete text of *Thomas* in 1945.[5] They are the parables of the Children in the Field (21), the Woman and the Empty Jar (97), and the Killer (98). The other stories in *Thomas* are different versions of the parables known already from the Synoptic Gospels: the Net Thrown into the Sea (8), the Sower (9), the Mustard Seed (20), the Weeds in the Field (57), the Rich Man (63), the Feast (64), the Vineyard (65), the Pearl (76), the Leaven (96), the Lost Sheep (107), and the Hidden Treasure (109). *Thomas* does not designate these narratives as parables, but clearly treats them figuratively. Unlike other sayings by Jesus in *Thomas*, the narratives are introduced by comparative frames, which liken the narrative to something (kingdom of heaven, kingdom of the Father, the kingdom, the Man) outside the narrative. The use of comparative frames applied to narratives is the characteristic way narratives are generally turned into figures in the Synoptic Gospels.

Thomas regards all discourse by Jesus as cryptic and challenges the reader to seek its hidden meaning, but the author does not introduce every saying with comparative frames. The placement of saying one at the beginning of the collection ("Whoever finds the interpretation of these sayings will not experience death") serves as a comparative frame for the entire collection, and it influences readers to seek a hidden meaning in every saying. The comparative frames introducing the parables in *Thomas* appear to be traditional, and this suggests the collector of *Thomas* did not append them to the narrative.

Parables in the *Secret Book of James*

The *Apocryphon of James* (*Secret Book of James*) gives a list of seven parable titles—the Shepherd, the Seed, the Building, Lamps of the Virgins, Wage of the Workers, Silver Coins, and the Woman (8:6–10)—but it does not describe their contents.[6] The author simply names them as though an informed reader would easily evoke their contents from memory. Three new narratives, unknown to the canonical tradition, also appear in *Secret James*, none of which is designated as a parable. A comparative frame, likening the narrative to something outside of it, introduces each, however: for example, "Don't let the kingdom wither away. For it is like a date palm shoot . . ." (7:22–25); "For instruction is like a grain of wheat . . ." (8:16–17); "For the kingdom of heaven is like a head of grain . . ." (12:22–23). Each new narrative, as well as the named "parables," is clearly regarded as a type of obscure discourse in need of clarification, because the text makes a clear distinction between "speaking in parables" and "speaking openly": "I first spoke to you in parables and you did not comprehend; now I speak to you openly and you do not understand" (7:1–6). The *Secret Book of James* is certainly clear that parables have more to them than meets the eye, and it treats them as allegorical figures whose interpretations are difficult to comprehend by both the outsider and the readers of *Secret James* (7:29–35; 8:23–27; 12:27–30). The parables may describe some aspect of the natural process, but hidden within is a religious message. The story about the ear of grain goes this way:

> The kingdom of heaven is like a spike of wheat that sprouted in a field. And after it ripened, he [the farmer] sowed its fruit, and again filled the field with wheat for another year. (12:22–27)

The interpretation reads:

> You also hasten to reap for yourselves a spike of life that you may be filled by the kingdom. (12:27–30)[7]

"FIGURES" IN THE GOSPEL OF JOHN

Like *Thomas*, John does not use the word "parable." Perhaps more significantly, John has none of the stories that the Synoptic Gospels, *Thomas*, and the *Secret Book of James* present as a characteristic form of Jesus' discourse. This is all the more interesting, since Mark says Jesus never addressed the crowds except by using (narrative) parables (Mark 4:33–34). Instead, John portrays Jesus as employing deliberately obscure figures or images, labeled *paroimia*.[8] In John 10:1–6, for example, Jesus uses the image of the sheepfold, which the narrator labels a "figure" (*paroimia*, 10:6) that no one understood. Images in John are extended, rather than compact, but they are not the typical narrative parables of the Synoptic Gospels. Other extended images are the vine and branches (15:1–8), the door of the sheepfold (10:7–10), and the good shepherd (10:11–18). These figures are described as deliberately obscure language in need of clarification. John quite consciously makes a contrast between figurative language (obscure or deliberately difficult) and plain language. Jesus says:

> I have said these things to you in figures [*paroimia*]; the hour is coming when I shall no longer speak to you in figures but will tell you plainly about the Father. . . . His disciples said, "Ah, now you speak plainly, and not in any figure." (John 16:25, 29; author's translation)[9]

WHAT IS A PARABLE IN EARLY CHRISTIAN LITERATURE? SOME CONCLUSIONS

From this brief survey, the obvious answer to the question "What is a parable?" appears to be: *A parable is any saying of Jesus that struck the writer of an early gospel text as an enigma or a banal saying, or any saying whose plain surface meaning does not yield an adequate religious concept.* This definition seems clear from the fact that a given saying may be "parabolic" or not, depending on who is using the saying. For example, Luke describes the aphorism about a blind man leading a blind man as a parable (6:39), and Mark designates as a parable Jesus' saying about a man being defiled by things coming out of him rather than going into him (7:14–15; cf. v. 17), and even provides the saying with a parabolic interpretation (7:18–23). Matthew, on the other hand, uses both these sayings in the same context (Matt 15:10–20), but for Matthew only one is a parable. In Matthew, Jesus speaks the defilement saying (15:10–11); the disciples explain that the Pharisees were offended by the saying (15:12). Jesus replies with two different sayings (15:13–14); the second saying is about a blind man leading a blind man (15:14; cf. Luke 6:39, where it is a parable). When Peter asks for an explanation of "*the* parable" (singular), the explanation following (15:16–20) relates only to the saying about defilement (15:10–11). The saying on the blind leading the blind (15:14) and the saying about the rooting up of plants (15:13) are apparently regarded as plain discourse. Neither the author of Matthew nor the character Peter in Matthew's narrative regarded the saying on the blind man as a parable.

The saying on wineskins and patched garments, shared by all three Synoptic Gospels, is another example. Luke 5:36–39 describes as a single parable what is easily recognizable as two sayings, each with different content (5:36 and 5:37–38), and follows the dual sayings with an interpretation (5:39).

Matthew 9:16–17 and Mark 2:21–22 do not seem to regard the two sayings as having a figurative character, and present them as simple discursive speech whose meaning is apparently self-evident, or at least the evangelists do not seem to think their readers will be confused by them. Matthew and Mark use them as simple images explaining why his disciples do not fast (Matt 9:14; Mark 2:18). Thus, modern readers of the gospels should not too quickly assume that what one gospel presents as a parable with figurative significance is also so regarded by the other gospels.

Another example, the Unclean Spirit, is neither designated a parable by Matthew (12:43–45) and Luke (11:24–26), nor do they treat it as a parable by introducing it with a comparative introduction. Only Matthew appends an interpretation to it. Because it shares an identical form (i.e., it is a story with a narrative plot) with the characteristic stories of Jesus described as parables elsewhere in early Christian literature, some scholars regard it as a parable.[10] Brandon Scott and Dominic Crossan apparently do not.[11]

STRATEGIES USED BY SCHOLARS IN READING PARABLES

Early Christian literature uses a variety of literary forms figuratively. Modern scholars have given them specific designations, depending on both form and content: proverb, image, metaphor, symbol, simile, similitude, and narrative parable. Metaphor and symbol do not have a distinctive form but are categories scholars use for describing how stories function. Allegory is both a literary form and a strategy applied to nonallegorical narratives.

A *simile* is a figure that uses "like" or "as" or some other comparative expression to liken two distinctly different things; for example, "Woe to you scribes and Pharisees, hypocrites! For you are like whitewashed tombs" (Matt 23:27). There are comparatively few similes in the gospels.

A *similitude* is a simile elaborated with some detail. Such comparisons are distinguished from similes or simple figures only by the increased detail in which the word picture is painted. Examples of similitudes given by some scholars are: Matt 13:33; Luke 14:28–33; 17:7–10. Others, however, regard similitudes as narrative parables with less detail, since they exhibit the basic elements of narrative in having a beginning, middle, and end. Matthew 13:33, although only a brief sentence, has a beginning, middle, and end, and is usually regarded as a narrative parable.

A *metaphor* does not have a distinct literary form, but many scholars think narrative parables function as metaphor. Metaphor is the use of a concrete incident from everyday life to express an abstract concept. Put another way, it is a figure of speech likening one thing to another specific—but unlike—thing by speaking of the one as though it were the other. In short, metaphor is a figure of speech describing one thing under the guise of something else. When the poet W. B. Yeats said, "An aged man is but a paltry thing, a tattered coat upon a stick" ("Sailing to Byzantium"), he was talking about old men as scarecrows. The real subject of Yeats's poetic line is old men; the vehicle used to carry this unstated concept is the description of the scarecrow. Likewise, some brief images in the gospels are thought to be metaphors. For example, Mark 2:21–22 records two sayings about concrete things that some think express abstract concepts. On their surfaces, however, these two sayings describe commonplace and routine activities in Palestinian antiquity: patching an old garment and storing wine. Those regarding these sayings as metaphors understand the concrete activities to be vehicles carrying specific abstract concepts. The abstract concepts are not stated since metaphor describes the abstract concept *as if it were* patching old clothes or storing wine. If these are metaphors, however, the inventor of the metaphor had a specific abstract concept in mind.

A *symbol* is exactly what it is, and something more besides. For example, if I say, "A shaggy brown dog is rubbing its back against a white picket fence," I am talking about a dog and a fence, and am presenting an image. If I say, "Some dirty dog stole my wallet," I am not talking about a dog, but am speaking metaphorically. If I say, "You can't teach an old dog new tricks," I am talking about both dogs and people, and am speaking symbolically.[12] Symbols are abstract concepts shared in community, and they have to be learned in order to be effective. The "something more besides" characterizing a symbol is difficult to quantify with certainty.

Symbols are quite imprecise and very rich in content; they potentially have a variety of meanings to different persons. The same image may symbolize different things to different people in the same community, depending on their learning and experience. For example, the Confederate flag until recently was the state flag of South Carolina. For many white citizens of the state it symbolized pride in the cultural heritage of the South. But for most black citizens of the state, on the other hand, it symbolized something vastly different—slavery, inhumanity, and degradation. Unless the writer has clued in the reader, it will be impossible to recognize with certainty that some statements are symbolic.[13]

An *allegory* as a literary form is a text that says one thing but intends that something else be understood. In the allegory nothing is what it appears to be. Elements in the allegory are ciphers with hidden meanings, which are not derivable from the words themselves; only in the imagination of the author or reader do these elements become other things. In one sense an allegory contains extended multiple metaphors, which deliberately equate numerous objects, persons, and actions with other things outside the allegorical text. Thus, a deliberate allegory actually represents many different things in the guise of other things.

John Bunyan's *Pilgrim's Progress* is a deliberate allegory.[14] Bunyan's hero, a man named Christian, represents every Christian believer, and Christian's journey chronicles the common vicissitudes of the Christian experience. Bunyan's allegory is thinly disguised (if at all), in which names, places, and experiences have clear meanings other than those they have in Bunyan's story about Christian. In the gospels certain parables are thought to have allegorical features, having been modified in the oral period of the Jesus tradition in order to make them more suitable for Christian interpretation. Compare, for example, Mark 12:1b–9 with saying 65 in *Thomas*, where Thomas's version represents a nonallegorical story and Mark the allegorized version. The evangelists have subjected other stories in the gospels to allegorical interpretations. Mark, for example, interprets a farming story (4:3–8) as a description of the hazards of Christian evangelism in the first century (4:14–20). Many modern scholars adopt an allegorical strategy for interpreting the parables and read them as allegories.

Dominic Crossan reduces these multiple forms (proverb, simile, similitude, parable) to three: aphoristic parables, extended parables, and narrative parables.[15] His third category he regards as the "most famous" parable; it is what people regularly study under the rubric "parable." By virtue of its literary plot and narrative form, the parable is clearly distinguishable from all others in the "parabolic discourse" attributed to Jesus. Crossan's description of Jesus' parabolic discourse does not include a category for the proverbs, which the gospels treat as aphorisms rather than as what they actually are—nonreferential community wisdom.[16]

ANSWERING THE QUESTION "WHAT IS A PARABLE?"

The answer will depend on the extent to which one builds on the gospels' view of parables. The three options in this regard are: (1) Assume the gospels are correct and parables are what the gospels say they are, without worrying about a consistent theory of parables. The difficulty with this solution is that the gospels are not describing literary forms but are using the word "parable" as a hermeneutical strategy. (2) Regard the literary forms identified as parables in the gospels as part of a "parabolic discourse," as Crossan suggests, and study aphoristic parables, extended parables, and narrative parables separately and together. The difficulty with this solution is that it ignores the gospels' designation of proverbs as parables. Crossan, quite rightly, does not have an "aphoristic proverb," since proverbs are not aphorisms. If the gospels are incorrect about one form, however, they may also be about another. (3) Examine each literary type independently. The third option will be followed in this book as the only reasonable approach to the literature. So, for example, the "parable" of the Laborers in the Vineyard (Matt 20:1b–15) will not be described as a "similitude," but rather as a narrative (or story) that has been transformed into a similitude by two hermeneutical appendages, Matt 20:1b and 16. The rationale is the form should be described as what it is, rather than on the basis of Matthew's strategy in presenting it to the reader.

Thus, in this book a parable is construed as a brief, freely invented, narrative fiction, comprised of beginning, middle, and end, dramatizing a common human experience or some incident from nature. The definition of what a parable is should not be confused with the question of how parables function. That is a different question and will be taken up later in this book.

2

Where to Begin?

First Steps in Reading the Parables of Jesus

Certain issues should necessarily be resolved before engaging the parables. The first step was to decide what to study. As argued above, the classic parable form is a story having a beginning, middle, and end. Some parables have more detail than others, but all have the basic ingredients of plot. In short, a parable is not simply a saying; it is narrative. Answering the question of how parables work is the second step, and also the most divisive issue in the study of parables today. An answer to this second question should be developed out of the parables themselves. Several other significant preliminary issues also need resolving before study begins. How they are resolved determines the character of the explanation of a parable.

Do Literary Settings and Interpretations in the Gospels Provide Information about How Jesus Used the Parables?

Do they provide historical information about the parables in the social context of Jesus (i.e., its setting in actual life) some forty years or so earlier than our written sources? Some scholars, perhaps many, will answer emphatically yes, while others will say absolutely not. For example, Joachim Jeremias thinks Luke's literary context (Luke 15:1–2) preserves "the original situation" in which Jesus told the parable of the Lost Sheep (Luke 15:3–7).[1] Because Jeremias generally disregards the literary settings of parables as products of the fertile imaginations of the gospel writers, his judgment must be regarded quite seriously. Jeremias has written the definitive history of parables interpretation, tracking their transmission from original utterance of Jesus to their written form in the gospels.[2] One conclusion, growing out of his analysis, is that "the primitive Church provided the parables with a [literary] setting."[3] Today Jeremias's insight that the literary framework of the parables does not represent the original social context of Jesus is the place where modern study of parables begins. By definition they are *literary* contexts—not eyewitness recitations of an original *social* context. Brandon Scott, for example, asserts we will never discover "a single actual, real situation of the parable," by which he means the specific social context that prompted a parable.[4]

Clearly this critical issue should be resolved in a separate step before addressing any parable. Reasons for treating the literary context as the social context must be stated. Because Jeremias's historical reconstruction of the parables tradition receives broad general support, exceptions require historical and literary arguments to the contrary. For many, however, a historical question becomes an issue of faith. From the perspective of their high religious view of the gospels, many are simply reluctant to attribute the literary settings of the parables to the inventive creativity of the evangelists. They decide the issue a priori based on what their faith holds about the gospels rather than on the results of literary and historical analysis. For about seventy years, scholars have taken the literary settings to represent the views of Hellenistic Christianity in the latter half of the first century, while the parables themselves, for the most part, represent traditional material, antedating the composition of the gospels. It is unlikely that a unanimous resolution will be achieved on this issue. At the very least, however, all those explaining parables should set out their historical rationale for regarding literary contexts as evidence for the public career of Jesus.

The contention of this book is that literary settings in the gospels represent later Christian interpretations rather than a historical memory of the original social context. Here is the reason: Each parable is a self-contained story, a little narrative world in itself. The literary introductions and conclusions are not part of that narrative world but evaluations of it, generally using words and concepts that do not appear in the story. Thus, the literary setting constitutes a particular early Christian strategy for reading the story. Without the influence exerted by the literary setting, the story is subject to multiple readings (i.e., it is polyvalent or polysemous). By embedding the story in a particular literary setting, the evangelists attempt to control the polysemy of the story (i.e., its potential number of plausible multiple readings), and in so doing they privilege their interpretation rather than the story itself. If the goal of reading is to understand how early Christians read the parable, then, by all means, one should begin with the evangelists' interpretations. If the goal is to engage the parable, however, then one should begin with the parable.[5]

The first step is to disengage the story from its literary context. Here is an example of how to do that. Embedded in Luke 18:1–6 is a brief narrative g a widow seeking a hearing before a judge. Only statements and es happening within the parameters of the interaction of judge and w are part of the parable's world. Hence, the narrative world of judge d widow is confined to Luke 18:2–5. Luke 18:1, 6–8 occur in a different world—that is, in the context of Luke's story about Jesus, in which Luke's character Jesus tells the story about a judge and widow to the disciples (cf. 17:22). According to Luke's Jesus, the story is an encouragement to pray, a statement that turns the widow into the hero of the story—that is to say, we are to be incessant in prayer like this widow, who keeps on coming to the judge in spite of his rebuffs of her pleas. Thus, the message of the parable is that one should never lose heart (18:1) or faith (18:8). This reading, on Luke's part, requires a subtle allegorical association: The widow represents a Christian woman abandoned in the world at the Lord's death; she is encouraged to be faithful and long-suffering in prayer, steadfastly looking for the Lord's return (18:7). Unfortunately, under such a scenario, God is forced into the role of the "unrighteous judge" who ignores the pleas of the plaintiff—or if stated in terms of the allegory, God disregards the prayers of the faithful.

Luke's interpretation is more readily apparent as part of the postresurrection crisis produced in the church some years after the Lord's death.[6] Lacking the value judgments placed on widow and judge by Luke's reading, these characters can be seen in a rather different light. The widow is not asking for justice but is demanding vengeance; the judge appears to be a thoroughly honest man who does not decide cases based on his religious faith but rather on the merits of the case. At the end of the story, however, he *considers* deciding the case not on its merits but for his personal convenience.[7] A judge in Israel who did not make judgments based on Torah would naturally be seen as "unrighteous" (18:6). Further, the widow is not "pleading" her case. Luke's interpretation turns the widow's strident "petitions" for vengeance into prayer and her persistence into steadfast faith. Luke arrived at such an interpretation by taking certain aspects of the story as hooks for his own theological agenda. Only in Luke's mind do they exist in the story, however. In this way, introductions and conclusions, provided by the evangelists, close off open engagement with the parables.

Does an Interpreter's Summary Truth or Moral Conclusion to a Parable Actually Capture the Irreducible Essence of the Parable, or Does It Represent a Particular Reader's Response?

The question poses a significant theoretical problem, discussed in more detail later in the book. Literary critics know that summaries or morals of poems and narratives are different from the poems and narratives themselves.[8] In short, the poem presents an experience of the poet, and it communicates to the reader in its own way. A prose summary or paraphrase of the main idea of the poem is not the poem itself—that is, it is not the experience of the poet, which the poem is (even if the author of the poem provides the summary). Only the poem itself provides access to the poet's experience. The summary and the paraphrase are narrative *responses* to the poet's experience. The same thing is true of the parables of Jesus, since they, like poems, are artistic (poetic) creations from his mind and experience.[9] A work of art, once completed, is independent of its creator's intention, and, in the final analysis, people evaluate it on the basis of their own experience.[10] In Amos Wilder's words, "It remains itself and goes on testifying or celebrating, independently of its interpreters."[11] So it is with the parables of Jesus. Interpreters and interpretations come and go, but the parables remain the focus of interest.

Polyvalence describes an innate ambiguity found in all narrative, a feature facilitating multiple responses (or meanings) from readers.

Here is an example of a parable provided with summary morals, which work against the polyvalence of the parable itself. Parables, like poems and other objects of art, are subject to a variety of readings if they are not closed off by interpretations limiting the reader's engagement with the story. The parable of the Lost Sheep appears in three versions in early Christian literature (Matt 18:10–14; Luke 15:3–7; *Thom* 107). Matthew's literary context (chap. 18) and interpretation (18:14) inform the reader that the parable is about God's ability to *keep safe his own*. The sheep that strayed is a "little one," and "little ones" are, in effect, disciples. Matthew addresses the entire chapter in which the parable appears to the community of faith.[12]

Luke, on the other hand, finds a different message in the parable. The Lukan literary context (Luke 15:1–2) and interpretation (15:7) inform the reader that the parable is about God's ability to *save lost sinners*. The lost sheep in Luke's story represents one lost person, whose recovery brings more joy to heaven than the Christians who have already repented (i.e., the ninety-nine sheep left behind). Luke has probably revised the parable, with an allegorical flourish, to emphasize the heavenly rejoicing over finding the lost sheep/sinner (15:6). Thus, in both interpretations, the shepherd takes on the character of a God figure who recovers wayward Christians and saves lost sinners.

Thomas has no interpretation, but the concluding line of the story (107.3, "I love you more than the ninety-nine") subtly implies an interpretation. It explains why the shepherd left the ninety-nine in the wilderness, something omitted from the stories in Matthew and Luke. In *Thomas*, it was the most valuable sheep in the flock.

If readers are not influenced by the summary interpretations to regard the shepherd as a God figure and the sheep as wayward disciples/lost sinners, the story takes on an entirely different character. Reading the story for itself and not looking for hidden "messages," the story is subject to a range of plausible readings. For example, Matthew's story appears to be about a risk-taking shepherd who daringly left ninety-nine sheep without supervision on the hills to search for one stray. I say "daringly" because the one sheep went astray while he was watching the flock. How many more sheep might wander away in his absence? So Matthew's story is about a risk-taking shepherd—or possibly a careless or irresponsible shepherd. He allowed one to wander away while he was watching, and now he exposes his entire flock to a greater risk in order to search for one stray. To judge the character of the story responsibly, a reader must know a great deal more about sheep farming, shepherds, and sheep in the first century.

Luke's story, on the other hand, is, rather clearly, about an irresponsible shepherd. In Matthew, the shepherd is only potentially irresponsible. His behavior can be seen in several different lights. Luke's shepherd, immediately after finding the lost sheep, returns home to celebrate the finding of the lost animal with friends and neighbors, irresponsibly leaving the ninety-nine alone in the wilderness. There is no other word for it.

In the *Thomas* version, the narrator appears to have been bothered by the shepherd leaving the ninety-nine to search for one stray, and thus gives a reason for the shepherd's behavior. He left the ninety-nine to go searching because the stray was the largest sheep in the flock, and he valued it more than all the rest put together. This conclusion casts the shepherd in an entirely different light. He appears to be a rather stupid shepherd, who does not understand the economics of farming. No matter how small the ninety-nine sheep were individually, their cumulative size and value would have been considerably greater than the one large stray. The behavior of Matthew's shepherd just might, under certain conditions, be commendable—sometimes risks are necessary—but the actions of the shepherds in the other stories are simply deplorable.

The way Matthew and Luke contextualize their stories clearly shields readers from the story's polyvalence. Far from capturing the "irreducible essence" of the parable, their different religious morals appended at the end actually work against the story. By casting the shepherd as a God figure, Matthew and Luke, in effect, ensure that the character's behavior in the story will be seen in the best possible light, while the stories by themselves cast him in a vastly different light.

What Is the Value of Noncanonical Parables?

Many scholars consider all early Christian literature as part of the raw data for analyzing Christian origins. Others, however, regard noncanonical literature as simply inappropriate for their study of *orthodox* Christian origins. The choice of data signals the difference between the historian and the dogmatic historian. The historian is interested in reconstructing Christian origins, and thus he or she studies all related historical data. The dogmatic historian is only interested in canonical data contributing to an understanding of orthodoxy. Data that falls outside the canon is ignored. Dogmatic historians privilege canonical literature over noncanonical. Hence, they conclude a priori that canonical versions of the parables are the most reliable. It is possible, however, that some versions of noncanonical parables have been shaped less by the authors of the texts in which they appear than have the versions in the canonical gospels. At the very least, noncanonical versions may alert the reader to revisions of the parable by the canonical evangelists. In principle, such a possibility may not be discounted, unless the reader rules, without investigation, that noncanonical versions are, in principle, less significant than the canonical versions.

In some cases, noncanonical versions of canonical parables actually appear to be simpler and less theologically developed. For example, *Thomas*'s version of the parable of the Vineyard (saying 65) is clearly less developed along allegorical lines than Mark's own version (Mark 12:1b–9).[13] In 1936 (prior to the discovery and publication of the Coptic *Gospel of Thomas*), C. H. Dodd conjectured what the parable of the Vineyard might look like without the allegorizing flourishes in Mark's version.[14] The parable in *Thomas*, published almost a quarter century later, provided striking confirmation of Dodd's judgment by its similarity to Dodd's reconstruction.

Thomas tends to be ignored by dogmatic historians, who cite what they regard as the relatively late date for the composition of *Thomas*—not earlier than 140 C.E. as they see it. The evidence argues, however, for an earlier dating of *Thomas*. The original editors of the fragments (representing three different versions of *Thomas* and not then recognized as such) dated the composition of *Thomas* not later than 140 C.E. (the inscription of the fragment Papyrus Oxyrhynchus 1 was dated not later than 200), and the editors held open the possibility that the composition of the original could be as early as the first century.[15] To put the matter in perspective, the earliest fragment of any canonical writing, a fragment of the Gospel of John (John Rylands Papyrus 457 = P52), is dated "in the first half of the second century."[16] Surprisingly, part of the rationale for dating it that early was by comparison to another noncanonical gospel, Papyrus Egerton 2.[17] If the critical date for the composition of the Gospel of John is within the first century (90 C.E.), there seems little reason to deny that dating to *Thomas*. In fact, the arguments for dating the Greek fragments of *Thomas* given by Grenfell and Hunt, the editors of the fragments,[18] have not been overturned, and no convincing rationale for dating the fragments later has been advanced in the discussion.

Actually the dating issue is a red herring, since all texts from the first and early second centuries had access to the same traditional material as the canonical gospels. Thus, in principle, a noncanonical version may be simpler and less theologically modified than the parallel canonical version, as was the case above with the parable of the Vineyard. Even if the noncanonical text in which a parable appears is later than the canonical version, it should not be disqualified for study. At the very least such versions can alert the reader to the hermeneutical trajectory of the parable, and that information can aid in critiquing the canonical versions or, perhaps, even in identifying an originating structure for a parable in cases where multiple versions of the parable exist in independent texts.

The parable of the Lost Sheep appears in three different versions: Matt 18:10–14; Luke 15:3–7; and *Thomas* 107. A close parallel analysis reveals striking differences. For example, a comparison of Matthew's setting (spoken to disciples) explains Matthew's interpretation—not one little one (disciple) will be lost (18:14). In Luke, the parable is told in defense of Jesus' association with tax collectors and sinners, and in this context the conclusion relates to the salvation of the lost (15:7). These different settings may very well explain why the sheep "goes astray" in Matthew (18:12) and is "lost" in Luke (15:4). Each evangelist has adjusted the parable to fit the context. *Thomas* has no literary context or appended theological conclusion; in *Thomas*, the sheep "went astray," which is what sheep usually do—they are prone to wander off. Thus, Matthew likely preserves a more original reading.

Matthew's story ends when the shepherd finds the stray. In Luke's story, however, when the shepherd finds the lost sheep, he does not go back to his flock. Rather, he leaves the ninety-nine in the wilderness and returns home to have a celebration with his friends and neighbors (Luke 15:5–6). The *Thomas* conclusion agrees with Matthew's; the story ends when the shepherd finds the sheep. The problem of what happened to the ninety-nine, left unresolved in Luke, does not exist in Matthew and *Thomas*, since there the story ends with the finding of the sheep. Again, it is likely Matthew who preserves an earlier version of the parable. If Matthew's version can be compared to Luke's, there seems to be no good reason for not comparing each to *Thomas*'s story as well—unless some a priori prejudice exists against *Thomas*. Surprisingly, however, there are still studies of the parables that ignore the comparative historical data *Thomas* provides,[19] or that simply note and then disregard *Thomas*,[20] or that treat the new parables in *Thomas* as gnostic creations,[21] or that in their analysis do not admit *Thomas* into the discussion on an equal footing with the canonical gospels.[22]

The new parables found in *Thomas* and the *Secret Book of James* have as strong an attestation as canonical parables attested in only one independent source. Thus, they have as high a claim to originality as parables with single attestation in the canonical gospels. The fact that scholars can read them from a gnostic perspective does not resolve the issue of their origin, since even canonical parables have been read from a gnostic perspective.[23] The fact that they appear only in later noncanonical sources is not sufficient reason, in itself, to exclude such parables before detailed analysis. If later texts cannot contain early tradition, everything in the canonical gospels will have to be excluded, since they were written a generation after the events they report. The only logical conclusion is to regard noncanonical versions of the parables as parables of Jesus—at least potentially so—and to study them as carefully as the canonical parables.

Did Jesus Use Allegory and Symbol as It Appears in the Hebrew Bible and Rabbinic Literature?

In Hebrew Scripture only a few narratives resemble the characteristic story parable typical of Jesus in early gospel literature. Those that do are narratives with plot. Ezekiel 17:2–10 (the Eagles and the Vine) is an allegory (*mashal*), followed by an allegorical interpretation (17:11–21), similar to the parable of the Sower (Mark 4:14–20). Ezekiel 19:1–9 (the Lions) and 19:10–14 (the Trees and the Bramble) are narratives, but are described as lamentation (*qinah*) rather than *mashal*. Judges 9:8–15 (the Trees and the Bramble) is a fable (a short tale in which animals or inanimate objects speak) that serves an allegorical function in the context. Second Samuel 12:1–4 (the Ewe Lamb) is a story functioning as an allegory. Second Samuel 14:5–7 (the Wise Woman of Tekoa) is a brief fictional narrative (14:1–3 shows its fictional character) used neither comparatively nor figuratively. Ecclesiastes 9:14–15 is a brief story (the Besieged City) followed by a summarizing moral on the superiority of wisdom (9:16). In their realism, these last three narratives are most like the typical parable of the early Christian gospels. Not all stories in the Hebrew Bible are used allegorically or figuratively.

In summary, the Hebrew word *mashal* is used to describe both narratives (Ezek 17:2–10) and brief figures (Ezek 24:3–5), which are given allegorical interpretations; traditional proverbs (Jer 23:28; 1 Sam 24:13; Ezek 18:2), which are given allegorical interpretations; lamentations that are brief narratives (Ezek 19:1–9, 10–14); and sayings (Hab 2:6; Mic 2:4). In general, *mashal* appears to describe any literary unit whose meaning is not immediately clear and easily understood, or it is a saying thought to hold some hidden significance (Pss 49:4; 78:2; Prov 1:6)—just as the evangelists present the parables of Jesus. In the Septuagint (the Greek translation of the Hebrew Bible), used by the writers of the gospels, the Hebrew word *mashal* is regularly translated as *parabole* (parable).

Some (e.g., Young and Blomberg) argue that Jesus used stories as *mashal* in the same way that they are used in the Hebrew Bible and in later rabbinic literature.[24] The major difficulty with using the rabbinic parables to explain the function of the parables of Jesus, however, is the late date of the written sources—some two hundred to five hundred years after the time of Jesus.[25] Some rabbinic parables, however, have been dated within the New Testament period (not necessarily the time of Jesus); a more specific dating for these parables is uncertain.[26]

Parables functioned for the rabbis both allegorically and metaphorically, according to Scott. He adds, however, that the parable genre "is neither by necessity allegorical, nor by necessity metaphorical. . . . Jülicher's categorical rejection of the possibility of allegory in Jesus' parables is unwarranted."[27] Scott does not take the next logical step, however, and conclude that in form parables as a genre are not necessarily figurative. The classic parable of Jesus is narrative, and narrative is subject to a wide range of uses. Narratives can be whatever narrators or authors want them to be: didactic stories, metaphors, allegories, symbols, moral lessons, or examples of proper or improper behavior. Narratives have no morals, and are a willing servant of any master.

The question "What use did Jesus make of his stories?" should not be resolved on the basis of how others in antiquity used them. The use of narrative in the Hebrew Bible and rabbinic literature does not, in and of itself, determine how Jesus used his stories. *Thomas*, for example (dating from the first century to the first half of the second century), provides neither allegorical interpretations nor summarizing morals to the parables of Jesus, as is also true even for some of the parables in the canonical tradition.[28] To assume that the parables of Jesus work like the *mashal* in the Hebrew Bible and rabbinic literature resolves the issue of function on the basis of an assumption. This approach puts the cart before the horse, so to speak, and privileges social context over narrative. Besides, there are closer parallels to the stories Jesus told, considerably older than the rabbinic parables,[29] and some closer in time to Jesus.

AESOP'S FABLES AND JESUS' PARABLES

In the light of the growing recognition of substantial Hellenistic influence on Palestinian Jewish culture in the first century,[30] it is worth calling attention to the fables of Aesop (the Latin *fabula* means "story") as potential literary parallels for the parables of Jesus.[31] Fables have a long history in the ancient Greek and Roman worlds.[32] Phaedrus (first half of the first century C.E.) and Babrius (second half of the first century C.E.) provide the classic collections, but each collector/editor used earlier collections in making his own.[33] The fable is generally described as a story featuring animals and inanimate things acting with human characteristics, but the collections feature other kinds of stories as well.[34] In contrast to the rabbinic use of parables, the fable is not allegorized but generally concludes with a brief moral. Moreover, not all the stories are unrealistic in their action. Among the fables attributed to Aesop are several stories bearing a striking similarity to the classic parables of Jesus in their realism. They involve the realistic action of human beings, do not have mythical elements or animals that speak, do not have a concluding appended interpretation (called an *epimythium*), and do not have an interpretive introductory statement (called a *promythium*). These appendages to the narrative are later devices telling the reader how to understand the story,[35] just as the canonical gospels do with parables of Jesus. The major formal difference between Jesus' stories and the realistic stories attributed to Aesop is that Aesop's frequently conclude with a gnomic sentence uttered by the last speaker, who, in turn, verbalizes the moral of the story.

> Here is an example of a realistic story ending with a gnomic sentence:
>
> An old woman saw a wine jar that the drinkers had left empty; but from the Falernian lees, still lingering in its noble shell, it spread forth a delightful odour. Eagerly she sniffed it up with all her nostrils, then exclaimed: "Ah, sweet ghost, how good you must have been before, when even your remains are so excellent!"
>
> Anyone who knows me will tell you what this refers to.[36]
>
> Phaedrus deliberately leaves the "moral" of the fable ambiguous or obscure.

Here are three fables closely resembling the characteristic parables of Jesus. They do not conclude with a gnomic sentence, but, like many of Jesus' parables, have been provided with a concluding *epimythium*:

> A man already in middle age was still spending his time on love affairs and carousals. He wasn't young anymore, nor was he as yet an old man, but the white hairs on his head were mixed up in confusion with the black. He was making love to two women, one young, the other old. The young woman wanted him to look like a young lover, the old one like one of her own age. Accordingly, on every occasion the mistress who was in the prime of her life plucked out such of his hairs as she found to be turning white, and the old woman plucked out the black ones. This went on until each of them presented the other with a bald-pated lover by the pulling out of his hair.
>
> [Aesop told this fable in order to show how pitiable a man is who falls into the hands of women. Women are like the sea; which smiles and lures men on to its sparkling surface, then snuffs them out.][37]

> A traveler who had a long way to go vowed that he would offer up to Hermes one half of anything he might find. By chance he came upon a wallet in which there were almonds and dates and he picked it up thinking that it might contain money. After shaking it out and finding what was in it he ate the contents; then taking the shells of the almonds and the pits of the dates he put them on an altar and said, "Here you have, Hermes, the payment of my vow; for I have shared with you both the outsides and the insides of what I have found."
>
> This fable is timely for an avaricious man who hoodwinks even the gods on account of greed.[38]

> A rich man came to live next door to a tanner. Being unable to endure the bad smells, he continually urged his neighbor to move, but the tanner kept putting him off by saying that he intended to move in the near future. This often happened, and it came to pass, as time went on, that the rich man became accustomed to the bad smells and no longer troubled his neighbor about it.
>
> The fable shows that habit tempers even the vexations of troublesome affairs.[39]

These stories, for which Aesop is given credit, reflect a close similarity to the stories of Jesus in brevity and realistic human action. They represent human beings realistically engaged in the course of common life in Hellenistic antiquity; they reflect no evident moralizing or allegorizing; they do not conclude with a gnomic sentence; like the parables of Jesus, the issues raised in the narratives are only partially resolved; and their application is left open.[40] The *fabula* is a very old and distinguished form in wisdom literature and is at least as promising a venue for contextualizing the parables of Jesus as the rabbinic literature and Hebrew Bible, if not more so, because of the dating problems with rabbinic literature. No problems exist with dating the fable, as it antedates Jesus. No problems exist with accessibility of fables to first-century Palestine, since they were widespread throughout the early Roman Empire. In this connection it is worth noting that a fable of Aesop is attributed to Jesus in *Thomas*: "Woe to the Pharisees, for they are like a dog sleeping in a manger of oxen; neither does he eat nor allow the oxen to eat" (saying 102).[41] Another *Thomas* parable, the Wise Fisherman (saying 8), is likely a Christian adaptation of an earlier fable of Aesop, the Fisherman and the Fish.[42] The general similarity of both versions (Aesop and *Thomas*) to Matthew's parable suggests that it too in some respects shares a tradition history with the fable of Aesop.[43] These parallels indicate the general flexibility of the Aesopic tradition in the ancient world.

Are the Comparative Frames to Parables Originally from Jesus, or Do They Derive from Early Christian Hermeneutics?

A comparative frame is a statement setting up a comparison between a parable and some other entity outside the parable.[44] The usual comparative frame is a dative construction: "As it is with [the situation in the parable], so it is with the kingdom of God/heaven." Joachim Jeremias argued that this Greek expression in the gospels derives from an original Aramaic expression, and, on that basis, postulated that it was characteristic of the historical Jesus. The comparative frame, however, could derive as easily from Aramaic-speaking Christianity, which presumably had as much difficulty with Jesus' stories as did later Hellenistic Christianity.[45] The usual element compared to a parable is the kingdom of God/heaven. The importance of this issue is highlighted by the fact that the only connection between the kingdom of God and the parables is precisely the comparative frame, which introduces less than half the extant versions of the parables of Jesus. It is quite possible that the author of Mark is responsible for first making the association between parables and the kingdom.[46]

Actually, a double problem lurks in the question that introduces this section: First, do the comparative frames derive from Jesus? Second, did parables without comparative frames originally have them? Only thirty parables out of a corpus of sixty-four are introduced by comparative frames.[47] Thus, less than half of all versions of the parables have comparative frames of any sort.

How should this data be evaluated? There are only four options: (1) The comparative frames, and lack of comparative frames, in the gospels are traditional; the gospel writers only wrote the information they received from the oral tradition or their sources.[48] Thus, parables were transmitted in the oral period, some with comparative frames and some without. It is not possible to know how they originated. (2) All parables originally had comparative frames. Some frames were lost during the oral period or omitted by the evangelists. (3) No parables originally had comparative frames. The frames to the parables in the gospels were supplied by the evangelists to make adequate religious sense of them. (4) The present relationship between comparative frames and the parables, as it exists in the gospels, represents exactly how they originated with Jesus. No changes were made to the parables, in this regard, in oral transmission or by the evangelists.

At present no consensus exists on the significance of the comparative frames introducing some of the parables. Scholarly practice, in the absence of debate and consensus, is inconsistent. For example, some scholars completely ignore the issue and treat all the parables as metaphorical figures of the kingdom, even those parables the gospels do not treat figuratively or even associate with the kingdom.[49] For others, the comparative frames encourage an allegorical treatment of all parables.[50] Others reject the idea of referencing and deliberate imagery altogether in spite of the figurative use of some of the parables in the gospels.[51] Others are more traditional; they privilege the evangelists' appended Christian moral (*epimythium*) over the comparative frame and reference to the kingdom.[52] Still others allegorize parables that have morals provided by the evangelists.[53] Before engaging the parables, interpreters should take a position on the issue of the comparative frames, setting out their historical rationale clearly.

Before beginning the study of a parable, some deliberated decision on these matters should be reached and communicated to the reader, along with the historical and literary rationale for the conclusions.

3

Is Jesus Really the Author of the Parables?

The Problem of Sources

Jesus actually "wrote" nothing attributed to him in the gospels; however, he is regarded as the originator of the parables. That he did "originate" most parables is a consensus among New Testament scholars—some would say all parables originated with Jesus.[1] Actually, the parables are regarded as the most certain of all the sayings attributed to Jesus. New Testament scholars are surprisingly confident the parables originated with the first-century historical man Jesus of Nazareth.

There is much more to the story, however. What we encounter in the early gospel literature are aspects of the historical man refracted through the lens of early Christian faith, and under those circumstances some distortion inevitably takes place—not the man *exactly*, but the man as early Christians believed him to be. Nothing concrete ties the historical man to the gospels, except the faith of the gospel writers and early Christian tradition. Thus Jesus, the historical man,[2] is a presupposition to the parables; he is their presumed inventor. As a presupposition to the parables associated with his name, Jesus is their theoretical first originator.

There are two reasons for thinking of Jesus as a presupposition to the parables, one historical and the other theoretical. The historical rationale is based on the observation that nothing in early Christian tradition comes directly from Jesus. To begin a study of the parables with the earliest physical evidence for Jesus necessitates beginning in the third century, because virtually all manuscripts of the gospels date from the beginning of the third century and later.[3] In the main, scholars think that the gospels were composed much earlier, namely, in the latter half of the first century. The earliest date any of the canonical gospels (Matthew, Mark, Luke, John) could have been composed is 70 C.E.

or shortly thereafter. The reason is because they mention the destruction of the Jewish temple, which occurred in 70 C.E. at the hands of the Romans.[4] Some scholars, however, date the gospels earlier, around 65–70 C.E., on the assumption that Mark (or Jesus) predicted the destruction of the temple (Mark 13:1–2).[5] The earliest date for the composition of the gospels that may be verified with complete certainty, however, is one that follows the destruction of the Jewish temple. Arguing that the evangelists, or Jesus, predicted the destruction of the temple—and using that argument to date any of the canonical gospels earlier than 70 C.E.—for the secular historian becomes special pleading, and for that reason is suspect. Such arguments do not produce unequivocal evidence. Historians will date a given document later than the events it describes, on the logical assumption that an event could not be described before it happens. The latest date for the composition of the canonical gospels is around the middle of the second century, when it becomes clear that the New Testament canonical gospels were known by name as written documents by the early church.[6]

The Gospel of Mark is generally thought to be the earliest gospel.[7] It was composed, according to current theories, out of discrete bits of oral tradition: sayings, sayings collections, brief stories, dialogues, and an account of Jesus' passion. To Mark goes the credit for providing these extraneous materials with a narrative framework. Matthew and Luke are later, and, in part, they used Mark's Gospel as a source.[8] For parables study, this means the parables that Matthew and Luke share with Mark are, in general, later versions of the Markan parables. Oddly, the Gospel of John has no parables.

During the years between the crucifixion of Jesus (around 30 C.E.)[9] and the composition of the gospels, traditions about Jesus lived in the memory of the initial followers of Jesus and later in the early Christian communities to whom the earliest followers passed on the traditions. They interpreted, revised, supplemented, and transmitted the sayings of Jesus and stories about him.[10] In short, the Jesus tradition belongs as much to the Jesus movement and the church as it does to Jesus himself. The result of this uncontrolled process is a tradition that frequently disagrees.[11] For example, in Mark's Gospel Jesus refuses to give a sign when it was requested of him (Mark 8:11–12). In Matt 16:1–2, however, when requested to do so, Jesus gives the "sign of Jonah," but he does not explain what it signifies. In Luke also, Jesus offers the sign of Jonah (11:29) but explains that the sign was the preaching of Jonah—that is, just as people repented at the preaching of Jonah, so they were repenting at the preaching of the Son of Man (Luke 11:30–32). In Matt 12:38–42, again Jesus offers the sign of Jonah when he is asked for a sign, but this time with two interpretations. One interpretation of the sign is the preaching of Jonah (as in Luke), and the other is Jonah's three days in the belly of a great fish. For Matthew, Jonah's stay in the fish signifies the Son of Man's entombment. In a remarkable contrast to the synoptic tradition, however, in the Gospel of John the entire public career of Jesus is filled with various signs (see the use of "sign" in John 2:11, 18, 23; 3:2; 4:54; 6:14, 26, 30; 10:41–42; 11:45–48; 20:30–31). Because of differences like these among the gospels, scholars are forced to ask how much of the tradition comes from Jesus, how much from the early Christian movement, and how much from the evangelists themselves.

A Jewish man named Jesus stands behind the early Christian traditions; he is their point of origin in some sense. What can be known of him, however, must be reconstructed from gospels written about him decades later. No Christian writing contemporary with Jesus' own day exists. Several different constructs of his career exist in the later gospel literature. The description of Jesus by contemporary Christian orthodoxy is a modern construct, ultimately deriving from what one segment of the early Christian movements thought of him toward the end of the second century. The orthodox construct glosses over the remarkable diversity among the early Christian accounts of Jesus.

As a consequence, a definitive profile of the first-century historical man is obscured to a great extent behind the theological descriptions of his career produced by the early Christians.[12] Though we see his shadow and may identify aspects of his career with some confidence, the historical man is largely concealed from the curiosity of the modern historian; he is the necessary presupposition to the Christ of the New Testament, the faith of its writers, and the parables attributed to him. In the New Testament, faith triumphs over history.

The theoretical reason for regarding Jesus only as a presupposition to the parables lies in the recognition that speakers and writers do not have absolute control over their words and literary creations, particularly in this case where a generation of oral transmission separates the first audition of the parables from their first inscription.

The value of knowing about an artist's life in order to understand his or her literary creations (literature, painting, sculpture, etc.) is debated, specifically by literary critics, and particularly with regard to poetry. On the one hand, some argue that knowledge of a poet's life is helpful for understanding autobiographical allusions in a poem. Others argue that a poem has integrity completely apart from what the poet may have intended.[13] In short, the author's intended meaning is not necessarily the same thing as what the poem itself communicates to various readers. Poet Wallace Stevens observed:

> I think that the critic [of poetry] is under obligation to base his remarks on what he has before him. It is not a question of what the author meant to say but of what he has said. In the case of a competent critic the author may well have a great deal to find out about himself and his work. This goes to the extent of saying that it would be legitimate for a critic to make statements respecting the purpose of an author's work that were altogether contrary to the intentions of the author.[14]

Stevens is simply saying that an author's work generally says more than the author intended to say.

Intention is a force that drives the artist toward a goal and guides the shaping of the artistic expression. The product, once completed, however, has life apart from its creator; the artist's intention, if known, becomes merely one standard among many on the basis of which the art is appreciated and critiqued. Two questions can at least be raised: To what extent does the artistic product in its finished state reflect the artist's intentions (if known), and to what extent does its finished state limit a potentially wide range of human responses to it? In other words, can the artist's intention control the polyvalence of the artistic expression? In the case of the parables, of course, it is impossible to know definitively the "artist's" intentions. All we have are parables. So in one sense, it really doesn't matter what Jesus intended; what really matters is the parable, the product of his creative mind.

Thus it does not matter whether we can conclusively identify Jesus as the originator of the parables or not. A collection of parables exists, and the parables can speak for themselves. Because the early Christians valued them as stories told by Jesus, for that reason they become interesting to historians of Christian origins and particularly to the church. In another sense, perhaps it is a good thing that there is some distance between who we think Jesus was and the parables, since our religious views of Jesus as the Christ should not be allowed to control how the parables are read. They should be allowed to witness to the historical man in their own way.

But in the light of this ambiguity as to their authorship, it is a fair question to ask: Why should the parables be described as the bedrock of the Jesus tradition? Several historical observations lead me to the conclusion that Jesus originated the parables. Independent strands of the written Jesus tradition point to Jesus as their originator. Mark, *Thomas*, *Secret James*, and the hypothetical sayings gospel Q all independently of one another identify Jesus as the originator of the parables. The fact that we have such a large number of parables (at least thirty-eight) for which no authorship other than Jesus is attested argues that Jesus originated them. While the brief stories Jesus seems to have popularized are certainly not unique to Jesus, their distinctive character argues for a singular creative mind. The similar forms found here and there elsewhere in antiquity (viz., Hebrew Bible and Aesop's stories) only emphasize the rather special character of the collection attributed to Jesus. And finally the stories attributed to Jesus bear the stamp of Palestinian culture and not the Hellenistic culture of the authors of the gospels who preserved them and who had so much difficulty understanding them. Such considerations as these successfully challenge the idea that Jesus did not originate the parables.

4

Why Did Jesus Speak in Parables?

Surveying the Literature

Through the years, my students have uniformly regarded stories as an excellent and effective means of teaching. When I ask them the following question, "Why did Jesus speak in parables?" they have a ready answer: Jesus was a master teacher and used parables because they are the most effective way to teach and communicate ideas. Nothing, however, could be further from the truth! Stories are ambiguous and subject to varieties of responses and interpretations, depending on how the individual auditor hears them. Unless the narrator tells auditors what they are supposed to take away from the story, auditors are left with an open-ended narrative, subject to a variety of explanations.

Here is an example of a modern story, a "parable" as it were, to illustrate the ambiguity of narratives:

> A certain man received a letter from the IRS. He took it to his accountant to review in order to draft a reply to the IRS. The accountant, however, was arrested three days later for embezzling funds, and the man was left to solve the problem himself. Because he was late in his reply to the IRS, he was subject to a large penalty.

I have told this and similar stories to my students, informing them that they will be tested on the story, particularly as to its moral, its point, or its message. Noticeably this story, like those Jesus told, has no *epimythium*, concluding gnomic sentence, or interpretation of any sort. Further, it has no formal context, other than the following: It is told in a formal academic setting, each student has an individual life experience on which to draw, and the story itself imposes certain limits on its interpretation.

As might be expected, responses are rather diverse. Some students focus on the formal context and assume that I, as a college professor, am looking for some ethical moral—we are, after all, in a college classroom. Thus, not unreasonably, they conclude that the story teaches the moral of self-reliance: The man who submitted the tardy report should have done his own work, rather than depending on the accountant. Others, not implausibly, focus on the final interest penalty and turn the narrative into a story about judgment: Both the accountant and the man who hired him broke the law and will suffer the appropriate penalty for their respective crimes. Other students find a religious moral, drawing on a judgment theme: Your sins will be punished in the end; you cannot escape the judgment of God. This last interpretation finds a subtle allegory in the story by reading the IRS as a God figure.

It is even possible to read the narrative as a fully developed allegory. The IRS represents God, who requires an accounting of every person. The man who consults the accountant is everyone who does not come directly to God with unresolved sin and life failures but who tries to accommodate them in other ways. Such persons find out too late that they must inevitably face the judgment of God. The narrative can even be understood as an example story, describing an account of negative behavior, and, thus, "the meaning, or thought or reality with which the story is concerned is not pointed to but is present in the story."[1] If it is an example story, it simply cautions people not to act in this way.[2]

Actually, the story was not created to do any of these things. It is a freely invented fiction told for the purpose of illustrating the polyvalence of stories. I had no particular meaning or moral in mind when I invented it. For me, the inventor, the story means what it says—no more, no less. Yet the story, once created, becomes independent of its creator and, as narratives are wont to do, it seduces auditors and readers. Potentially, I suppose, the story could mean almost everything said about it above, even though I invented it for entirely different purposes. However, the interpretations are related to the story in varying degrees of plausibility, but no less so than the interpretations we find to the stories of Jesus in the gospels. And how can I, the inventor, deny the invention's own testimony? Such interpretations are caused by the story's polyvalence when auditors and readers engage it. What I "intended" with the story is only one possible way the story may be heard, and maybe, in the final analysis, it is not even the best possible way.

WHY DO PEOPLE TELL STORIES?

The reasons can be as varied as the people who tell them. For example, a joke with a beginning, middle, and end is a story told for the purposes of humor. If the humor has an edge, the joke could be intended as humorous libel, a racist remark, or any number of other things. For example, a racist joke may be intended to demean through sarcastic humor by playing to a stereotype. Other stories are told for the purposes of entertainment—a ghost story on a cold winter's evening during a sleepover, for example. Others are told to stress a particular point or illustrate something. The reasons stories are told may be as numerous as the people who tell them.

The fable was described in chapter 2 as a near first cousin to the parables of Jesus because it was closest to the parable in terms of brevity, form, content, and realism. Since Jesus is the only parabler we know in Greco-Roman antiquity, it is, therefore, not unreasonable to inquire why fables were told.

The fourth-century B.C.E. Greek philosopher Aristotle included fables as a part of his discussion of the rhetorical tradition. Rhetoric was the art of persuasion with words—in other words, it was oratory[3]—and fables were regarded as part of the proof for achieving persuasion. Aristotle describes the fable as an invented example (*paradeigma*). He regarded it as more effective than examples taken from actual events, since the fable could be shaped to fit the proof being offered. Surprisingly, Aristotle also uses the word parable (*parabole*) to describe what we know as fable (*logos*).[4] The fable, as example, worked comparatively or, to use Aristotle's word, it worked parabolically.[5] By laying the invented fable alongside the principal issue, the truth depicted in the fable could be applied to the principal issue. Thus, a parable/fable was used to illustrate a particular truth.[6] Aristotle's study makes rhetoric sound like very serious business, and it was. Rhetoricians used their skills to compose pleadings and argue cases in court. Not all rhetoricians used their oratorical skills to serious ends, however; some saw themselves as entertainers. For example, one second-century writer, Lucian, was a traveling orator, who went from place to place speaking on various topics. "He was not a philosopher nor even a moralist . . . [and] his mission in life was not to reform society nor to chastise it, but simply to amuse it."[7] He was, in short, a satirist who employed his considerable satirical skills to amuse his audience and readers.[8]

Theon, a late-first-century Greek writer, said that a fable was "a fictional story depicting a truth,"[9] and this became the standard definition in the rhetorical and lexical traditions.[10] The fable was told to communicate a particular "truth" depicted in the narrative. So this kind of literature, even if it were occasionally humorous, was intended ultimately to be serious, and was generally equipped with *promythia* and *epimythia* to specify the moral and ethical truths the fable was thought to depict.

Phaedrus, the first-century writer and collector of fables, gives the following reason for collecting and publishing fables:

> A double dowry comes with this, my little book: it moves to laughter, and by wise counsels guides the conduct of life. Should anyone choose to run it down because trees are vocal, not just wild beasts alone, let him remember that I speak in jest of things that never happened.[11]

So throughout the Hellenistic period, brief fictions, even of a moralist type, were invented and told for a variety of reasons.

WHY EARLY CHRISTIAN WRITERS THOUGHT JESUS USED PARABLES

Jesus of Nazareth is portrayed in the Synoptic Gospels as a teller of parables, just as Aesop was portrayed as an inventor of fables throughout Hellenistic antiquity. Precisely why Jesus told parables is unknown. All that remains for the historian to ponder with regard to Jesus' intent are the parables themselves collected by his early Christian interpreters: Mark, Matthew, Luke, *Thomas*, and *James*. No primary sources from the time of Jesus give the historian direct access to his intent. There are, however, several reasons given in later Christian literature explaining why Jesus spoke in parables.[12] These explanations constitute the rationale of later Christians, a generation removed from Jesus, and are not to be directly attributed to Jesus himself—at least not without a historical argument to show the plausibility of such a thesis.

The *Gospel of Thomas* and the *Secret Book of James*, aside from the canonical gospels, are the only two early Christian texts dated in the first and second centuries having collections of parables. They do not address the issue of intent directly, but clearly they found Jesus' parables perplexing.[13] *Thomas* finds all of Jesus' sayings, not just parables, enigmatic.[14] So presumably, according to *Thomas*, things of significant value are contained in his sayings. In the final analysis, this means the parables are unclear on their surface and the things of value contained in them must be sought, but *Thomas* gives no reasons for their lack of clarity. The *Secret Book of James* presents the parables as deliberately arcane. They are a kind of disguised language, which is contrasted with open, or clear, language:

> At first I spoke to you in parables and you did not understand; now I speak to you openly and you do not understand. (*Sec. Book Jas.* 7:1–6)[15]

As if to emphasize the disciples' lack of understanding, Jesus later says he had to delay his ascension for an additional eighteen days "for the sake of the parables," presumably because the disciples still did not understand them (*Sec. Book Jas.* 8:1–4). Both *Thomas* and *Secret James* agree that the parables are difficult to understand because of their *nature*. They do not say why Jesus decided to use such a difficult medium, however. Presumably, he could have been more direct in his statements had he chosen to do so.

The situation is different in the canonical gospels. The earliest gospel, Mark, gives a precise reason why Jesus used parables. Jesus says to his disciples:

> The secret of the kingdom of God has been given to you. But for those outside all things are in parables, that seeing they may see and not perceive, and hearing, they may hear and not understand, lest they turn and be forgiven. (Mark 4:11–12; author's translation)

Thus, according to Mark, Jesus used parables to *prevent* everyone but his closest disciples from understanding him, because if they understood, they might "turn" and be forgiven. Under Mark's theory of parables, Jesus uses obscure language (parables) to keep people from experiencing God's forgiveness. Neither Matthew nor Luke agrees completely with this theory—nor do most church people and scholars today.

A COMPARATIVE ANALYSIS OF MARK 4:10–12; MATT 13:10–17; AND LUKE 8:9–10

Because of the surprising character of Mark's rationale for the parables, a close analysis of Mark and the parallel texts in Matthew and Luke is warranted.

Mark 4:10

The setting in each gospel: The segment begins in Mark with Jesus completely alone. In Matthew (13:1–3) and Luke (8:4), on the other hand, Jesus is apparently still in the presence of the crowds.

Mark: *Those about him with the twelve asked . . .*
Matthew: *The disciples came and said . . .*
Luke: *The disciples asked . . .* (author's translation)

Who is this shadowy group that asks the question in Mark? They are clearly disciples, or, at the very least, followers of Jesus in some sense, because Mark says the secret of the kingdom is given to them (4:11). In Matthew and Luke, the disciples are the interlocutors of Jesus; no such ambiguous group exists.

Mark: . . . *about the parables.*
Matthew: . . . "*Why do you speak to them in parables?*"
Luke: . . . *what this parable meant.* (author's translation)

In each text, the disciples ask a different question. The question in Mark is not specific but relates to all the parables. Matthew and Luke sharpen the question in different ways. In Matthew, the question goes to Jesus' motivation in using parables. In Luke, the disciples ask about only one parable, the Sower ("this parable," i.e., the one just spoken in Luke 8:5–8).

Mark 4:11

Mark: *To you has been given the secret of the kingdom . . .*
Matthew: *To you it has been given to know the secrets of the kingdom of heaven . . .*
Luke: *To you it has been given to know the secrets of the kingdom . . .* (author's translation)

In Matthew and Luke, the disciples are given the ability (i.e., it is given to know) to distinguish the numerous secrets (plural) concealed in the parables (cf. Matt 13:51–52; the competent disciple knows how to find these treasures). In Mark, however, there is a single secret.[16]

Mark: *. . . but for those outside, all things are in parables.*
Matthew: *. . . but to them it has not been given.*
Luke: *. . . but for others they are in parables.* (author's translation)

Mark's statement creates two groups—an insider group and an outsider group. The insider group, the Twelve and those about Jesus with the Twelve, is comprised of the disciples/followers of Jesus to whom the secret of the kingdom has been given. The outsider group is comprised of everyone else—specifically, the crowds Jesus addresses with his parables (4:1–2, 33–34). Matthew (13:11) parallels Mark rather closely. The secrets (plural) of the kingdom are given to the disciples, but not to the crowds, whom Jesus addresses in parables (13:11: "them" refers to the crowds found in 13:1–3 and 10). The sharp language of insider/outsider used by Mark (4:11) is missing, however. Luke also has two groups, but the distinction between them is not quite as sharp as in Matthew and Mark. In Luke, only the secrets of the kingdom are in parables. Thus, Luke seems to imply that the crowd will be able to understand some of the things Jesus says—just not the kingdom secrets. In other words, in Luke not everything Jesus says is in parables. The assumption seems to be that those other things might be understood. In Mark, on the other hand, since *everything* is in parables, only the disciples will understand, since Jesus explains the parables only to them (4:13). Nondisciples understand nothing, and Jesus does not want them to understand. Matthew shares Mark's exclusiveness, making the exclusion of the crowds complete in Matt 13:14–15. Their inability to understand (in Matthew only) is due to their own hard-heartedness—they have deliberately closed their ears to Jesus and refused to understand, as Isaiah said would happen (Isa 6:9–10, Septuagint).[17]

Mark 4:12

Immediately before he includes his own version of Mark 4:12, Matthew (13:12–13a) adds two additional statements not found in Mark 4:10–12. Matthew 13:12 is shared with Mark, although Matthew uses it immediately after Matt 13:11 and Mark uses it elsewhere (4:25). In Matthew's context, the statement seems to reinforce the idea that the secrets of the kingdom given to disciples are not given to the crowds ("them" in Matt 13:10). In fact, whatever inkling the crowds might have had about the true significance of the parables is taken away (". . . but whoever does not have [the secrets], even what he or she has will be taken away," 13:12b; author's translation), and those capable of understanding the secrets of the parables find their ability to understand enhanced ("to whoever has will more be given," 13:12a). Matthew is the only writer to address directly the reason Jesus spoke in parables: "For this reason I speak to them in parables . . ." (13:13)—because the crowds are fated to ignorance. The "prophecy" of Isaiah (Isa 6:8–13) is fulfilled in the crowd's response to Jesus (Matt 13:14–15; cf. Isa 6:10, Septuagint). In a sense, it makes no difference what Jesus says to the crowds. God has foreseen, and foretold through Isaiah, their deliberate rejection of Jesus. In Mark, on the other hand, Jesus uses parables *in order that they* (i.e., those outside, 4:11):

> may see
>   but not perceive
> may hear
>   but not understand
> Lest they turn (or in order that they not turn), and receive forgiveness.
> (author's translation)

Hence, according to Mark, Jesus deliberately uses language designed to keep people from understanding.

Luke's view is similar to Mark's but not as harsh. For Luke, only the secrets of the kingdom are in parables. These kingdom secrets in Luke's view are intended for the disciples. Thus, Jesus uses the concealing language of parables so that the crowds may see and hear but not really understand. Luke omits Mark's final offensive phrase about turning and being forgiven. Because it is only the secrets of the kingdom that are concealed in certain parables, such as the Sower, other things Jesus says—even in parables—may be understood.

EVALUATING THE HISTORICAL VALUE OF THESE TRADITIONS

In the latter half of the first century and early in the second century, the church was struggling to find satisfactory meanings for Jesus' parables that fitted its understanding of Jesus as Lord, and it was searching for its place as a historical entity in the Hellenistic world. Mark's solution to this problem is the earliest, at least according to current theories of Christian origins. Mark's view, simply stated, is: Jesus deliberately kept everyone but his followers from understanding by using parables. A few years later, Matthew was unhappy with this explanation and changed Mark's theory.[18] According to Matthew (13:16–17), only the church (the followers of Jesus) understands Jesus' parables. The rest of the world does not understand them because they have hardened their hearts, as Isaiah had foretold would happen. Luke thinks that only the disciples are privy to kingdom secrets, found in parables such as the Sower. Nondisciples may, however, be able to understand other things. Lack of knowledge of kingdom secrets will not keep people from turning and being forgiven. Thus, Matthew and Luke had no independent historical knowledge about why Jesus used parables. They simply edited out those things in the Markan theory they found most objectionable.

I know of no contemporary modern scholar who seriously entertains the idea that Mark was historically accurate in tracing his theory about the parables to Jesus.[19] Most regard the theory as Mark's own.[20] A few argue that the theory was traditional, that it antedated Mark but did not originate with Jesus.[21] Not everyone appears willing to take a position on the issue, however.[22]

The bottom line on why Jesus used parables is this: No one knows, and virtually no scholar believes that Mark knew what he was talking about in tracing his parables theory to Jesus. Even Mark's own theory fails in places. In one instance, for example, Mark indicates that nondisciples did understand a parable directed against them: In Mark 12:12, the chief priests, scribes, and elders understand that the parable of the Vineyard casts them in the role of the murderous tenants. In another instance, Mark's conclusion to the parables chapter (4:1–34) suggests that the crowds may have been able to understand the parables: Mark 4:33 says, "With many such parables he spoke the word to them, as they were able to hear it." "Them," also contrasted with the disciples in 4:34, refers to the crowds (4:2, 11, 21, 24). The final phrase in Mark 4:33 is not really clear, but it seems to hold open the possibility that as the crowds were able to understand, Jesus spoke to them in parables.[23]

Matthew, Mark, Luke, *Thomas*, and *Secret James* are primary source material for attitudes of the church in the latter first and early second centuries. Their description of the parables as deliberate arcane language intended to conceal describes how the church felt about parables when it came to distilling appropriate religious messages for its later institutional situation. Because of the obvious difficulties experienced by the church in understanding Jesus' Jewish stories as Christian stories, it is not surprising the parables were seen as containing deliberately encoded hidden messages and allegories.

ALL WE HAVE ARE THE PARABLES THEMSELVES

We are left with the parables, which make good sense when read as stories, but poor sense if the object is to find theological or allegorical messages in them. In the main, the parables are thoroughly secular, and realistic slices of first-century Palestinian life. When read for themselves, they give the impression that they are completely transparent. Their qualities of secularism, realism, and transparency work against the idea that they are opaque, encoded, arcane, and allegorical. The clear allegorical features in some few parables are more easily understood as secondary Christian allegorizing of realistic Jewish stories.[24] Allegorizing and moralizing of the parables constituted the church's hermeneutical strategy for getting around the secularism and realism of the parables. Recent developments in the study of the Bible and the ancient world, however, are focusing precisely on the social and cultural values of biblical texts in their historical-social context. These studies are helping to clarify the realism of the parable and the social contexts of the subject matter of the story.[25] With increased emphasis on such studies, a Christian rhetoric ignoring the realism and secularism of the parables (and the implications of these features) will be increasingly more difficult to maintain. The essential transparency of the parables as realistic first-century stories has yet to be addressed by the allegorists and those who seek for Christian morals.

5

What Do Parables Present to the Reader?

Realistic First-Century Fictions

Scholars have always been interested in the cultural environments of early Christianity: It was born Jewish and later nourished into a Greek religion independent from Judaism. Jesus and his first followers were Jews in every sense of the word, but the New Testament was written in the context of Hellenistic culture. Hence, scholars have studied the two social worlds of Christian origins—Palestinian Judaism and the Greco-Roman culture of the early Roman Empire. Only recently, however, have New Testament scholars begun to study Christian origins and New Testament literature through the lens of social-scientific methodologies.[1] Scholars who use social-scientific methodologies "attempt to explain Israelite and early Christian developments" by means of "concepts and models from sociology and anthropology."[2] In effect, they use the New Testament and related literature to reconstruct the social world of early Christianity and also to reconstruct early Christianity as a movement in that world. Reading New Testament texts in this way, rather than for theological reasons and spiritual insight, is warranted precisely because they are first-century texts that preserve realistic aspects of their culture, both deliberately and inadvertently.

REALISM AND THE PARABLES

Parables scholars have been aware since the late nineteenth century that the parables are essentially realistic narratives about village life in Palestine in the first century. Adolf Jülicher's basic point in breaking the monopoly of allegory on parables interpretation was "that the parables Jesus told give the impression of being vivid and understandable," that they are "vivid simple pictures, taken from real life." They are not "esoteric and mysterious," and they did not require explanation when Jesus told them in the first century.[3] C. H. Dodd, following Jülicher, found the parables to be similes or metaphors "drawn from nature or common life."[4] Jeremias, following Jülicher and Dodd, regarded the parables as stories "drawn from the daily life of Palestine,"[5] and he attributed the unrealism of allegory to an early Christian search for a meaningful Christian message in the parables.[6] Amos Wilder, the New Testament scholar who has done most to bridge the gap between literary concerns and New Testament study, said: "What is of special interest in the parables of Jesus is not only that he told stories but that these stories are so human and realistic. One can even speak of their secularity. . . . [T]he impact of the parables lay in their immediate realistic authenticity."[7] Finally, Norman Perrin's assessment of the parables of Jesus as essentially realistic first-century narratives has never been fully appreciated:

> The parables of Jesus are *occasional* texts; they were directed toward a specific group of people on specific occasions and they assume a whole spectrum of history, culture, and experience shared by the parabolist and his hearers. Jülicher and Dodd had developed the thesis that the parables were realistic pictures and stories, drawn from life. But the life from which they were drawn is the *petit-bourgeois* and peasant life of Palestine in the early Roman Empire. If we are to understand those pictures and stories historically, therefore, we must understand that life from which they were drawn.
>
> I [i.e., Perrin] would personally put a great deal of emphasis upon this last point. The parables of Jesus are pictures and stories drawn from *petit-bourgeois* and peasant life in Palestine under the early Roman emperors. They are not myths employing archetypal symbols; they are not fables exploiting the universal features of the human condition; they are not folk tales appealing to the collective experience of a people as a people. They are vivid and concrete pictures and stories drawn from the details of a particular situation at a given time and place. They are occasional, transitory, essentially fleeting snapshots of life.[8]

Perrin's criticism of Jeremias, who wrote the definitive history of parables transmission, and put parables scholarship on a firm scientific basis, serves as a warning to anyone who ignores the realism of the parables:

> The weakness stemming from Jeremias's concern for the voice of the historical Jesus is that ultimately he is not concerned with the parables as texts with an integrity of their own, needing to be interpreted in their own right. His ultimate concern is the message of Jesus as a

> whole, and the interpretation of the parables is for Jeremias only a means to the end of reconstructing this message. For all the time and effort that he has spent on the interpretation of the parables he is really only interested in them as contributing to an overall understanding of the message of Jesus. He does not respect their integrity as texts.[9]

Perrin is arguing that the realism of the parables and their integrity as autonomous texts in their own right should be taken seriously. This repeated emphasis in the secondary literature on first-century social world realism in the parables by such important figures in parables study is generally overlooked in the modern study of parables. If Perrin's caveat had been heeded, the direction of parables study would likely have taken a different turn in the last thirty years. Attention would have shifted from (theological) meaning in parables to the first-century Palestinian social world and aspects of first-century society reflected in the parables, for only that approach truly respects the integrity of the parable as historical narrative. If a parable is a realistic narrative "still life" or "snapshot" from peasant life in first-century Palestine, it should be read against that background.

A parable of Jesus is not, as many think, a "narrative fiction in which the agents and actions, and sometimes the setting as well, are contrived to make coherent sense on the 'literal,' or primary, level of signification, and at the same time to signify a second, correlated order of agents, concepts, and events."[10] The realism of parables denies that they are *contrived* fictions stressing some other playing field of literary, or theological, reality. Invented fictions they may be, but they are not fictions in which "meaning" is found in a "second correlated order" that controls the "primary level." Precisely because the parable re-presents aspects of a real world and imposes that world on the reader, it violates the integrity of the parable to look for meanings in a secondary level of reality, which the reader must imaginatively devise and foist on the parable. In other words, parables mean exactly what they say, and should be studied for what they are rather than for what readers take them to "signify." Their realism provides a control on overactive imaginations. The context for reading and evaluating them is common village life in first-century Palestine and not early Christian theology, faith, or morals. Parables represent a marriage of uncommon creative imagination with common aspects of first-century Palestinian life. "Respecting the integrity of the parables as texts," as Perrin puts it, requires a focus on their poetics, plots, and their representation of action in first-century Palestinian society. The realism of the parables challenges the theory that Jesus was working with a well-worn thesaurus of stereotypical plots and stock characters.[11] Parallels to the content of parables should be sought in first-century real-life situations, as these can best be reconstructed, for there is nothing really stereotypical about the actions Jesus portrays in his stories. As Perrin said, the parables are not folktales.

HOW REALISTIC ARE THE PARABLES?

Most of the parables portray common peasant folk engaged in average, down-to-earth activities. And even those parables featuring characters not of the peasant class portray them in actions true to their status in society.[12] On the whole, Jesus does not tell stories about kings and the trappings of royalty, but describes common folk caught in the act of being themselves. They are people in the local village—next-door neighbors to Jesus' auditors. For example, he describes a peasant farmer sowing a field and the kinds of hazards any small farmer faces at every sowing season (Mark 4:3–8, par.); a woman sweeping her house looking for a lost coin (Luke 15:8–9); the behavior of a particular man (not everyman) who unexpectedly finds a lost treasure (two versions: Matt 13:44 and *Thom* 109); a shepherd searching for a lost sheep (three different versions: Matt 18:12–13; Luke 15:4–6; *Thom* 107); a man hiring and paying day laborers (Matt 20:1–15); the haphazard planning and murder of a powerful man (*Thom* 96); the murder of a landowner (Mark 12:1–11; Matt 21:33–43; Luke 20:9–18; *Thom* 65); the questionable actions of a man fired from his job (Luke 16:1–7); and two bumbling farmers worrying with a fig tree in a vineyard (Luke 13:6–9). To appreciate the commonness of the stories Jesus told, see the categories under which Brandon Scott discusses the parables in his table of contents—family, village, city and beyond; masters and servants; and home and farm[13]—plus my own classification of the parables in terms of social, cultural, and economic facets of Palestinian society.[14] In the stories Jesus told, realism trumps theology. In the interpretations of the evangelists and the contemporary church, theology trumps realism—and has the final word.

A READING OF A PARABLE ABOUT A DYSFUNCTIONAL FAMILY

Here is an example of how the realistic language of Jesus trumps theology, when theological interpretations are not allowed to have the last word. Much ink has been spilled over the well-known and popular parable of the Prodigal Son. There is only one early Christian account, Luke 15:11–32, and it is something of an anomaly among the parables of Jesus for two reasons; it is the longest parable Jesus told, and it reflects two distinct plots: the prodigal son

(15:11–24) and the elder brother (15:25–32). Particularly the shift in focus away from the prodigal son to the elder brother has been problematical for some interpreters, who raise the specter that Luke may have composed the second half, while the first half is traditional.[15] The usual way the parable is read emphasizes the great love the father had for his wayward son. Some even see the father as a God figure.[16] The parable has been read in other ways, however.[17] If readers are not misled by Luke's literary setting (15:1–2) and on that basis read the story as Jesus' defense of his practice of eating with tax collectors and sinners (thus turning the father in the story into God), it is simply a tragic story of a dysfunctional family.[18] As is well known, dysfunctional families are not unique to modern society.[19]

The story narrates a particular incident in the lives of a father and his two sons, one younger and the other older. The narrator tells us nothing about a mother and sisters, if they even existed. Auditors/readers may speculate about them, but their presence is not required for this particular story to work. The father owns a farm large enough to require the presence of hired workers (15:17, 19)[20] and slaves (15:22). Further, his holdings were large enough that he could liquidate whatever portion of his "livelihood"[21] was slated for the younger son at the father's death (15:12)[22] and still have an estate large enough to require slaves (15:22). The farm was probably managed by the older son rather than directly by the father (15:22, 25–26).[23] The younger son asked for the share of the father's property "falling" to him, that is, the share of the estate coming to a younger son at a father's death. Apparently without batting an eye at the younger son's request (demand?), the father on the spot divided his living between both sons (15:12). Clearly the father had ultimate control of the estate, since he himself made the division. There is no indication that the father was obliged to do what the younger wanted; yet he immediately acceded without any further discussion. In the light of what subsequently happened to the younger son (15:13), the father's act was clearly unwise, and, at the very least, appears to be unusually permissive—the actions of a doting parent, a view somewhat borne out by the father's uncharacteristic behavior at the son's return from the "far country": "His father . . . ran and embraced him and kissed him" (15:20). Numerous commentators have described the father's running as uncharacteristic behavior for a head of household.[24] Nevertheless, unusual behavior is not unrealistic behavior. For example, Esau ran to greet Jacob on his return from "a far country" (Gen 33:1–4). The act of running to greet the younger son on his return seems clearly appropriate to the character of a permissive father. He did not even permit his son to make a proper confession, cutting it off before the son could complete what he had earlier rehearsed (compare 15:18–19 to 15:21). In short, "the father goes overboard"[25] in his reception of a son who had wasted the family's resources.

Scholars have been unable to find clear evidence that granting a son an allotted share of the family estate before the death of the parent was a generally accepted custom in Palestinian Judaism. The best advice cautioned against such an action.[26] The fact that there are cautions against such behavior, however, confirms that it happened under some circumstances. Nevertheless, customary or not, the parent in this story is portrayed dividing up his property between younger and older sons, and this act by the father is what eventually leads to the break between him and the older son (15:28–29).

The father apparently handled his younger son unwisely, and at the end of the story is doing the same thing with the older son. When the younger son abruptly turns up after being given up for dead (twice mentioned in the narrative: 15:24, 32), the father immediately throws a welcome home party (15:23)—without even bothering to tell the older son. Returning from the field, the older son hears the sounds of the party in full swing (15:25) and wonders what is going on. Only at that point does he learn for the first time, from a child,[27] that his father had thrown a party for the younger son (15:26–27). Naturally, the older son is thoroughly piqued at not being consulted, or even invited, and refuses to join the festivities. If Bailey is correct about the older son's role of "host" at such banquets, then the father's omission of the older son can only be read as an insult to the older son.[28] He simply took his older son for granted. He apparently thought so little of him that he had forgotten him in the excitement of the younger son's return. It was clearly an oversight on the father's part, as his later urging of the older son to join the party shows. The older son's complaint shows that this incident was part of a behavior pattern on the father's part: The father had never given him even so much as a kid for partying with his friends—much less the fatted calf—suggesting the father clearly favored the younger son. The father tries to placate the older son with the appropriateness of festivities at the younger son's rather miraculous reappearance (15:32), but he does not address the real complaints of the older son (15:29), namely, the father's preference for the younger (15:29)[29] and his failure to recognize the older son's long and faithful service to the family (15:29). Naturally the older son was agitated. There appear to be two sides to this family squabble.

The story describes an indulgent parent who pampers his younger son and slights the older. Basically, the father has not treated both sons the same, and he has personally created the dynamic leading to the crisis with which the story leaves the reader: An irresponsible younger son returns to continued pampering by an overindulgent father, and a responsible older son is now alienated from both of them.[30] An auditor/reader might well wonder how to situate himself or herself into the landscape of this rather depressing fictional story. All the characters are flawed, and the narrator gives no hint at a solution. The story ends unresolved. Action and dialogue seem quite realistic, if not even contemporary, and the broader social issues addressed by the story transcend any one time and place. Reading the story in this way makes it very difficult to see the story as theological pronouncement or promise.

This story of a dysfunctional family actually focuses on the father; he is the lynchpin that holds both parts together. In the dynamics of the story, however, he is not presented as an ideal character worthy of emulation. His inept handling of both his sons is too clear in the narrative to allow such a reading. Giving the younger son his allotment of the family estate before the father's death is the one social-world feature that helps to clarify the father's inept or permissive character, and it argues against making him a cipher for God. Such a practice undoubtedly existed in Palestinian antiquity because of the warning against it. Sirach 33:19–21 advises against it for the physical welfare of the parent-owner, but there seems little doubt that the emotional welfare of this particular father and his family unit would have been better served had he heeded the warning. Because the practice was not mandated by Jewish law or custom but was even warned against, the father's action raises the related questions of his judgment and his motivation for such unusual liberality. In the light of the way the story turns out, his judgment was clearly flawed, and this, in turn, forces the reader to see his unusual liberality as overindulgence. The social-world background forces the reader to acknowledge the father's unusual liberality as excessively permissive, which acts as a brake on turning the father in the story into a God figure.

THE SOCIAL WORLD OF THE PARABLES

The reader's initial question of a parable should not be "What did Jesus mean by that?" The history of parables scholarship is littered with the bones of contradictory and failed answers to that question; in the final analysis, it can never be answered definitively. Rather, the first question should be "What is going on in this narrative?" This approach aims at reconstructing from the story (and elsewhere) aspects of social life in first-century Palestine, and then aims to fit the parable into that context. Some of this research may seem rather banal to theologians who probe the parables in search of directions for contemporary Christian living, but it situates the parable in its natural habitat, which is the social life of first-century Palestinian Judaism (assuming the story actually was invented by Jesus, of course). Situating the narrative in that context helps to clarify the dynamics of its plot in its historical and social context.

A reader must engage the cultural world in which the parable was invented in order to hear it as its earliest audience might have heard it. The social facets and dynamics of that world may be strange, even foreign, to modern readers, but a first-century auditor would have understood subliminally aspects of the story escaping the modern reader. Such subliminal awareness operates in every culture. Persons who are strangers to the culture need to have explained to them what natives instinctively know without explanation. For example, in England where automobile traffic proceeds in the left lane, British natives know instinctively to look to the right before crossing a street. In the United States, where vehicular traffic proceeds in the right lane, natives know instinctively to look left before crossing a street. The lack of subliminal awareness on the part of visitors to England has prompted civil authorities to paint instructions ("Look right before crossing") on the curbs of streets in the major tourist centers to accommodate foreign visitors, who are accustomed to a different flow of vehicular traffic.

Similarly, the parables require knowledge of first-century Palestinian society, economics, politics, religion, and farming practices if they are to be understood in that context. Such knowledge of first-century practices evokes awareness of subtleties in the narrative missed by the heavy-handed searcher for theological ideas. For example, in his reading of the parable of the Laborers in the Vineyard (Matt 20:1–16), William R. Herzog suggests a different reading of Matt 20:13a.[31] The word "friend" used by the landowner to the day laborer objecting to the unfairness of paying workers equal pay for unequal work takes on a different tone in Herzog's reading. "The landowner is shrewd." He picks out the leader of the day laborers "and makes an example of him. . . . 'Friend' is not a friendly term. It is condescending and subtly reinforces their different social stations, yet it feigns courtesy."[32] Only because Herzog reads the narrative in its natural habitat, in the context of the economics of agrarian societies, can he sense the subtlety of this exchange between an elite landowner and a landless peasant. Knowledge of the social world acts as a brake to the overeager imaginations of all who mine the parables for theological insights. In this case, Herzog's unmasking of the character of the exchange between the landowner and the day laborer makes any identification of the landowner with God a near impossibility. Readers unaware of such almost subliminal social values are easily led astray in their readings. Would interpreters of the parable of the Sower (Mark 4:3–8) argue that the story turns on a bountiful harvest (Mark 4:8) if they knew that the harvest in the story is really only an expected yield for wheat?[33] Would readers of the Fig Tree in a Vineyard (Luke 13:6–9) be so quick to associate the owner of the vineyard with God if they were aware that the story casts the owner as a flawed character? The owner does not seem to know that fig trees were commonly used in vineyards for trellising grapevines, and he consequently tells the vintner to cut the tree down because he does not want it *uselessly* occupying space in the garden. If he wanted the tree removed, however, he should have told the vintner to dig it out, roots and all, since competent farmers know that stumps of fig trees will sprout if watered.[34]

The fact that parables are realistic fictions means three things for those who ponder parables. It means that a reader's focus should remain on, and in, the story. It means that the elements of the parable (characters, objects, and action) should be understood in terms of the story and in their natural environment—first-century Palestinian village life. It means that parallels to elements in the story are sought from a first-century social world. The realism of the story automatically eliminates any secondary plane of reality informing the parable, if the reading is to be construed as a historical reading.

6

What Does a Parable Mean?

Caveats to Readers of the Parables

How exactly do we imagine the process of arriving at an "explanation" for a particular parable of Jesus—or any other narrative, for that matter? The word generally used to describe the process, at least in traditional biblical scholarship, is "interpretation." When a parable is explained, it is interpreted, goes the conventional wisdom. The interpretation of the parable establishes *the* meaning of the parable—at least it does for that interpreter. Craig Blomberg, for example, entitled his book *Interpreting the Parables*; Brad Young entitled his *The Parables: Jewish Tradition and Christian Interpretation*; and George Shillington's title is *Jesus and His Parables: Interpreting the Parables of Jesus Today*.

Virtually all who offer explanations of parables will at some point in the discussion describe the process as interpretation. In this context, "to interpret" signifies "setting forth *the* meaning of." In other words, interpreters purport to provide the single authoritative "meaning" of the parable or other narrative. Of course, the word "interpretation," and its related forms, does not have to be used in such an exclusive way but can simply describe *an* explanation of a given parable—one among several equally plausible explanations.

Yet in the history of New Testament scholarship, the act of interpretation has functioned much more dogmatically. A given interpretation sets out the way readers *should* understand a particular parable—to the exclusion of other explanations. Interpreters tend to think of the process of parable interpretation as discovering some innate meaning in the words of the narrative itself, which may ultimately be tracked back to the mind, and intention, of Jesus himself. Usually an interpreter will reduce a parable to a particular summary statement, or paraphrase, which is conceived as *the* clarification of the parable's main thrust—much like the summary interpretations attached to parables in the gospels. Robert Stein, for example, asserts, "In seeking the main point of the parable [the Prodigal Son, Luke 15:11–32] we see the one possibility that immediately comes to the forefront is that Jesus sought to demonstrate through this parable the greatness of God's love and his willingness to forgive. . . . The parable teaches in beautiful simplicity what God is like, his limitless love, his boundless love, his amazing grace."[1]

On the other hand, Brandon Scott has carefully avoided the word "interpretation" to describe what he does in his book *Hear Then the Parable: A Commentary on the Parables of Jesus*. When he concludes his analysis, he provides "a reading" of the parable, signaling, it would seem, that more than one "reading" of a parable is possible.

> The fictive, narrative quality of parables bestows on it an independence of its *Sitz im Leben* [life setting]; as narrative with open meaning, parables can be used in a variety of situations. Thus we can distinguish two levels of meanings. Situational meaning is the particular meaning that a given real hearer or reader imparts to the text depending on his or her situation and context. But a secondary level, the literary level, concerns textual structuring, a semantics which is self-referential. To switch metaphors, this second level supports and is the condition for the first, for it provides the possibility of both multiple and specific application in the situation of Jesus and the narrative of the Gospels, and in subsequent readings.[2]

In other words, parables (narratives) by their very nature possess the potential of multiple readings (or explanations) and no *one* reading can claim to be the single authoritative reading to the exclusion of all others.

WHAT IS THE MEANING OF "MEANING"?

Language is actually unstable, and it resonates in different ways for different readers and auditors. In part, that is why readers and auditors find different plausible "meanings" in the same statement or narrative. Let's begin this discussion with a definition of the term. "Meaning" describes, in the final analysis, a particular reader's response to a given text. The term indicates how that particular reader responded to the narrative on the basis of his or her background, knowledge, values, and experience—that is, on the basis of the sum total of elements comprising the world of that particular reader. Thus, "meaning" does not innately inhabit a text, where readers must search for it, but meaning is created by an interaction between a particular reader and a text. Meaning is evoked, if at all, in the reader's mind; it inevitably originates in the nexus between the text and reader—where the reader's world intersects the text's world—for texts also have backgrounds and reflect knowledge, a sense of values, and an author's experience. Thus, an author decides what the text says, but readers decide what it means.

How is it that language is unstable? Narratives are comprised of words, phrases, clauses, and sentences, providing data that readers process. Let's take the smallest unit of a narrative as an example—words. What words signify to readers is contingent on a number of factors. The word *List*, for example, in the German language is a noun signifying cunning, craftiness, artfulness, artifice, device, stratagem, trick, ruse. In English, however, as a noun, "list" indicates a series of items written seriatim; a border or bordering strip; a strip of color; a division of the hair or beard; a ridge or furrow; a careening or leaning to one side. As a verb, "to list" indicates the process of setting forth items in a sequence; registering a security on a stock exchange for sale; offering something for sale, as in a catalogue; preparing ground for planting by making ridges or furrows; cutting away a narrow strip of wood from a stake; inclining to one side. There are also archaic uses of the English word. At one time, it meant to enlist; to be pleasing to; to please; to like or desire; to choose; to listen; to listen to.[3] These multiple significations for this one word should caution every reader that all words have an innate capacity for multiple significations. So the meaning of "list" depends on the language of the text in which it is encountered, the date of the text, the immediate context in which the word is found, and, most importantly, on the reader's linguistic abilities and preferences.

The multiple significations of words, in both spoken and written language, can be delimited by several controls: the cultural context in which the word is spoken and written; its syntactical use and immediate literary context; and the experience, limitations, and personal views of the reader. In an oral context, a speaker's intonation must also be considered as one of the variables controlling the stability of words. In short, words do not have a single inevitable meaning. Each is capable of a range of functions in a given language and in different contexts. Thus words, the building blocks of language, are only potentially meaningful to a reader. There is no way to control their instability so as to ensure one authoritative meaning for each that functions in every circumstance and context and excludes all others. It is only possible to limit the instability to some extent.

AMBIGUITY AND POLYVALENCE

These words mean essentially the same thing. In chapter 2, polyvalence was described as an innate ambiguity found in all narrative that facilitates multiple responses (or meanings) from readers. Ambiguity, created by the instability of words and gaps in a narrative, is also innate to narrative, and readers (or auditors) must resolve the ambiguity by stabilizing words and bridging the gaps as best they can in order to make sense of the narrative.[4] Readers will always find different ways to resolve the ambiguities and bridge the gaps. For example, in what I have called the parable of the Dysfunctional Family (Luke 15:11–32; see pp. 39–42), there occurs a crucial gap in the narrative at 15:23–26. The narrative neither makes clear why the father did not invite the elder brother to the feast in celebration of the younger son's homecoming, nor does it explain why the older brother became angry.[5] How a reader resolves these ambiguities in the narrative determines the nature of the story: Is it a story about a gracious father of two sons (as Stein's reading requires), or a story about a dysfunctional family? Most interpreters follow Linnemann, who argues that the gap is due to the narrator's stage management of the narrative.[6] The narrator deliberately left the gap to contrast again the father's generosity (he goes out to his elder son as he did with the younger) with the elder son's (churlish) refusal to join the celebration. Thus, the invitation to the elder son is omitted deliberately to contrast the father's generosity and the elder son's resentment of his younger brother (Luke 15:32).[7]

As with all gaps, however, this one may be filled differently. The father pleads with his older son to come to the feast (after it had already begun) because of the joy of the occasion (Luke 15:24, 32), and the elder son refuses. The elder son's problem is not with his younger brother; it is with his father. His monologue focuses on the father, not his younger brother: "I served *you* these many years, never disobeying *your* commands. Yet *you* never gave me a feast. But when *your* son who wasted *your* living returned, *you* gave him a feast." From the elder brother's perspective what is contrasted (in his monologue) is the father's uneven treatment of his two sons, one proven unreliable and the other faithful. Yet it is the unreliable son who is honored. When viewed in this light, the "stage management" is more easily explained as a reinforcement of the father's indulgence of the younger son and his benign overlooking of the older son.[8] In any case, because of the ambiguity, multiple explanations are possible. No authoritative final answer is ever really possible, because resolution is left to the readers.

Even texts without gaps are polyvalent. One interesting example is the rather opposite reading of Gen 15:6 by Paul and the author of the book of James. Paul read Gen 15:6 (cf. Rom 4:3; Gal 3:6) as proof that God had credited Abraham with righteousness because of his faith alone. Abraham was not justified by doing the works of the law, says Paul, but by faith in God (Rom 4:1–25; Gal 3:1–9). Abraham simply could not have achieved righteousness by observing the law, since the law was given later through Moses. James 2:18–26, on the other hand, argues from the same text (Gen 15:6; cf. Jas 2:23) that Abraham's faith alone was insufficient. Works are required to complete faith, argues James. Thus, Abraham was not justified before God until he had actually offered his son Isaac (Gen 22:1–19) as a sacrifice to God (Jas 2:18–24, 26). James concludes that people are not justified by faith alone; rather, certain kinds of behaviors are required for faith to be effective (2:24).

Matthew and Luke found enough ambiguity in the Q parable of the Lost Sheep (Matt 18:12–13; Luke 15:4–6) to understand it in directly opposite ways. For Luke, the parable relates to the salvation of sinners (Luke 15:1–3a, 7), whereas Matthew reads it as relating to the preservation of already believing disciples (cf. 18:6: "little ones who believe in me," cf. 18:10, 14). Even if both interpretations are construed to come from Jesus himself, the parable must still be conceived as polyvalent enough to accommodate both of these rather divergent readings.

The summary interpretations of Matthew and Luke do not resolve the ambiguity of the parable of the Lost Sheep. The parable responds favorably to still further readings.[9] The readings of Matthew and Luke are only possible by taking the shepherd as a figure for God. In Matthew, the shepherd is the Father who wills that all his "little ones" be preserved (18:14). And in Luke the shepherd is the Lord of heaven who brings even the least lost one into redemption (15:7). In order for each evangelist to make this association, the shepherd in the story must be viewed as responsible and caring. Such may be the character of God, but that is not an inevitable description of the character of the shepherd in the story. The actions of this particular shepherd actually call his character into question, an observation that is usually overlooked because the evangelists' interpretations make a subtle allegorical association of the shepherd with God. The shepherd in the story was actually irresponsible when he abandoned the ninety-nine sheep and exposed them to the dangers of the wilderness. Without the supervision of the shepherd, other sheep in the flock could wander off. If he lost one sheep while he was watching his flock, how many more might wander off when he is not watching? Without the shepherd's supervision, the flock is subject to carnivorous animals, which would decimate and scatter the flock (note the image in John 10:12–13).

Matthew's story stops with the finding of the lost sheep (18:13), so readers do not know what the shepherd found when he returned to the last known location of his flock. But Luke's shepherd does not even return to check the flock; he leaves the ninety-nine in the wilderness, while he returns home to celebrate with friends and neighbors his finding of the lost sheep (15:6). He leaves the ninety-nine in the wilderness with no supervision (those who assume he left them under supervision are writing a different story). What else other than irresponsibility would prompt a shepherd to disregard the safety of the entire flock, putting his entire livelihood at risk?

On the other hand, perhaps the narrative is actually commending the risk taken by the shepherd—and it clearly was a risk to leave the sheep alone in the wilderness. After all, one sheep was lost while he was watching—how many might he lose when they are not being watched? When viewed in this light, the shepherd is neither caring nor irresponsible; rather, he is a courageous and daring shepherd who is willing to place the remainder of his flock at risk in hopes of securing the whole. At least that may be true for Matthew's shepherd. It is very difficult to overlook Luke's ninety-nine left alone in the wilderness while the shepherd heads home to celebrate. Matthew's shepherd refuses to accept the certain loss of even one sheep, and daringly risks the remainder. The narrative affirms this reading to some degree, since the finding of the lost sheep is not certain (18:13: "if he finds it"). What would justify the risk? The narrative does not address that question, but some sheep might be quite valuable and thus justify the risk. In the *Thomas* story (saying 107), for example, the sheep that goes astray was the largest, and that is why the shepherd valued it so highly.

On the other hand, a daring act to one person may well be foolhardiness to another, and such readers are not likely to see Matthew's shepherd in a positive light. For them, Matthew's shepherd simply doesn't understand the economics of the situation: Ninety-nine in the fold clearly are worth more than one in the bush! Because the motivation of the shepherd is left ambiguous in Matthew and Luke, his character (caring, irresponsible, daring, foolhardy?) is left to the judgment of the reader. Only *Thomas* gives a motivation for the actions of the shepherd—he loved the largest sheep more than the ninety-nine.

INTENTIONAL AND AFFECTIVE FALLACIES

These two fallacies emerged from a challenge to traditional literary criticism (which biblical studies tend to be) in the first half of the twentieth century.[10] It was initially called "the New Criticism," but as other approaches developed toward the end of the twentieth century, it became known as "formalist criticism."[11] The New Critics, working with certain kinds of poetry and short stories, argued that everything a critic needed for judging an artistic work (poem, or short story) was present within the work itself.[12] Traditional criticism, on the other hand, argued that the critic should learn everything possible about the life of the artist, the artist's intentions, and the historical period in which the artist produced the work.

The New Critics countered that to judge a work by what the artist *intended* was clearly wrongheaded; what really mattered was what the artist *accomplished*. "Original i[ntention] and achieved i[ntention] are not the same thing and in most instances there is probably a considerable discrepancy."[13] In short, they argued that the work ought to be judged for what it was, and on its own terms. In this way the New Critics dismissed the intentions of the artist as a criterion for judging the work. Reaction to the "New Criticism" was mixed,[14] but the insight that the actual artistic work is not the same as the intended artistic work is cogent. A work ought to be judged for what it is, and on the basis of its own "organizing principle." The work of art itself "contains, insofar as it is a work of art, the reason why it is thus and not otherwise."[15] Thus, the intentional fallacy argues that the place to begin studying parables is with the parable itself, rather than with the intention of Jesus in inventing the parable—since we have no idea what that was.[16]

The New Critics also identified what they regarded as another critical error in evaluating artistic works, which they dubbed the "affective fallacy": evaluating a work of art based on its effect on the mind of the reader/viewer. The work exists independently of the critic's evaluation, just as it is independent of the artist's intention. The fallacy lies in assuming that the character of the work is the same as what the critic thinks it is.[17] Thus, readers of parables are cautioned not to assume that their interpretations of a parable accurately describe the character of the parable. Their readings are merely one response to the parable. The authority for controlling responses to a parable is the parable itself. While a reader may not be able to say what the authoritative reading of a parable should be, the parable itself rules out, to some extent, inadequate or inconsistent evaluations.

To illustrate the intentional and affective fallacies, I have selected a poem of my own composition. It is not offered as an example of a "good" poem, but only because it is possible for me to be certain about the author's intention in writing the poem.

Les plumes de la dent du lion[18]

Late in the orange and yawning evening
The tawny horde creeps in
By companies in battalions.
Their globular erect plumes shimmying
Erotically
In the steamy summer breeze
Swords bristling
Around bright green battlements.
Puffy papyrus chutes assault
Unsuspecting and still stretching greening

With olive projectiles rigid and penile
Thrusting continuously into the fertile front
Sortie after endless sortie
Exploding wave after endless wave.
Late in the orange and yawning evening
They fold their yellow guidons
Reviving flaccid stems
For the dawning
Aureole of early morning.

I was consciously writing a poem about dandelions, hence the title. The English word "dandelion" is derived from the French *dent du lion* (literally, "tooth of the lion"). The subject of the poem was the annual assault of dandelions in middle-class American lawns in the heat of the summer.[19] The poem was not intended to reflect any serious philosophical ideas, unless lawn care is judged a serious subject. I was describing an experience, namely, frustration with my annual summer battle with a pesky weed. I made a conscious choice to use colors in the poem (orange, tawny, green, olive, yellow, golden), stimulated, in part, because dandelion seeds are olive in color. I deliberately chose military language (horde, companies, battalion, swords, battlements, chutes, guidons) as appropriate to describe what I saw as warfare between me and the cursed weed.

I consciously introduced the word "erotically" to describe shimmying—but only intended that it should influence "shimmying," not thinking that its influence would reach any further. There are, however, other words in the poem, as I found out later from students, that evoked a sense of eroticism for the entire poem (erect, shimmying, steamy, rigid, penile, thrusting, exploding wave, flaccid, aureole), although the terms are completely understandable, and accurate, in terms of what I *intended* to accomplish in the poem—to provide a vivid description of the annual summer assault of the dandelions.

Assuming I am telling the truth—and that the reader believes what I have just written about my intentions and how I went about writing the poem—what should be said about this poem? Does what I intended to do with the poem become the final word for how the poem should be read? Or should one read the poem for what it is in itself? Can I, the author, insist that it is not an erotic poem because that was not my intention, even though some readers insist that the poem is deliberately erotic? People who think my intentions control the poem commit the intentional fallacy: finding the norm of the work in the author's intention rather than in the work itself.

On the other hand, readers, no doubt seduced (from the author's perspective) by the word "erotically" in line 5, are reading something into the poem that is really not there (or so the author thinks). The so-called erotic language is easily understood in terms of the description of the summer dandelion season. In this case, readers who find the poem erotic are basing this judgment on how it affects them, rather than on the poem itself, and are therefore committing the affective fallacy.

The first of these fallacies cautions the reader of parables that any study of a parable begins with the parable itself rather than with what they assume Jesus may have intended by it. The second warns that a reader's response to a parable should not be confused with the parable itself. The final authority for evaluating a parable is the parable itself.

How can the parable be the final authority for evaluating itself? That likely sounds like double talk to some readers, but it is nonetheless true. Parables (like poems) provide in themselves certain constraints to reading them; these are guidelines for how they should be read—general ones, to be sure, but they are there built in to the parable. There are at least four.

1. The realism of the parable undermines any reading disregarding its realism, and exposes for what it is the idealism of readings of the parable deriving from another plane of reality. Idealistic readings basically ignore the parable's realism. The parable puts all its cards on the table face up, and deliberately conceals nothing from the reader: A farmer is a farmer, a weed is a weed, a fig tree is a fig tree, a steward is a steward, a type of soil is a type of soil, and so on. Attempts to make them into something else suitable to another plane of reality are mocked by the transparency of the feature in its natural environment in the parable.

2. The language used in the parable establishes the limits of its discourse with the reader. Thus, readers are engaging the parable only so long as they observe the limits of its language world. When the reader uses language not authorized by the parable, the reader has broken off engagement with the parable and is in a sense talking to himself or herself. The reader is then describing a personal reaction to the parable, which may be based in ideas the reader has extrapolated from the parable but are not there as such in the parable. Such ideas come out of the reader's mind.

3. The parable is only interested in the social world of village life in Palestinian Judaism. When the reader strays out of the first-century village where the action of the story takes place, the reader has broken off engagement with the parable and is again talking to himself or herself.

4. The openness of the story invites the engagement of all readers. Since none of the stories of Jesus are closed off with authoritative interpretations *within* the story, their invitation to every reader is "What do *you* think about this situation?" Because the stories are constructed without a conclusion, the message to every reader is: No final authoritative readings to parables are possible. Trying to close off the parable with *the* authoritative solution must be

considered a literary heresy because it violates the story's basic construction. Thus, there will always be a range of plausible readings to every parable. And within these four guidelines parables will continue to solicit the engagements of readers to make discoveries about themselves and their world within the story.

THE HERESY OF PARAPHRASES AND SUMMARY INTERPRETATIONS

Poets recognize the value of students reading a poem and summarizing or paraphrasing it in order to come to a better understanding of what the poet is saying, but they quickly point out that the paraphrase or summary is not the poem.[20] The summaries and paraphrases do not re-present the poet's experience, which is the poem itself. Poetry (like short stories and novels) communicates an experience of the poet. Summaries, paraphrases, and messages found in the poem by readers do not do, and cannot do, what the poem does.

> The poet from his own store of felt, observed, or imagined experiences, selects, combines, and reorganizes. He creates significant new experiences for the reader—significant because focused and formed—in which the reader can participate and that he may use to give him a greater awareness and understanding of his world.[21]

The heresy, of course, is substituting a particular reader's summary or paraphrase for the experience of the poem itself.[22] The poet's experience, which is the poem, is much more than the summary.

Much parables study, beginning with the synoptic evangelists, has tended to fall prey to this literary heresy. The summarizing interpretation, the paraphrase, the main point, the theological teaching, and so forth all tend to replace the parable and control how readers experience it. The tail wags the dog, so to speak. Rather than facilitating the reader's experience of the parable, these "interpretations" tell the reader how to experience the parable, closing off a reader's free engagement with the parable. The parable is no longer open for readers to engage for themselves, as Jesus' original auditors had to do for themselves. Two thousand years of Christian theology works to control the parable and ensure that readers have the "right" experience.

PART 2

Strategies

7

Jesus the Figure Maker

Parable as Allegory, Metaphor, and Symbol

Persons who see Jesus as figure maker think that his stock-in-trade was nonliteral language. He said one thing with his stories but intended that auditors understand something very different; in other words, what he said was not what he meant. That is to say, the language of the parable meant something other than what it said. In short, his language was figurative. Figurative language is an "intentional departure from the normal order, construction, or meaning of words in order to gain strength and freshness of expression, to create a pictorial effect, to describe by analogy, or to discover and illustrate similarities in otherwise dissimilar things."[1] The uniform early Christian opinion about Jesus is that he was a maker of figures, and one primary way the parables of Jesus are read today is treating them as figures.[2]

ALLEGORY

Allegory is the oldest strategy applied to Jesus' parables; allegorical interpretation regards parables as repositories of many different Christian truths. This approach to the parables occurs in the earliest extant gospel, Mark, and still survives today as the principal way parables are read in the church.[3] An allegory is a narrative that tells one story on its surface but whose elements are ciphers, which, rightly understood, tell an entirely different story. In narratives that are unambiguously allegories, such as *Pilgrim's Progress*, the different story is reasonably obvious. The narrative's departure from reality, by using language in unusual ways, frequently gives away the fact that the story is not to be taken literally. In other cases, however, figurative language is not immediately obvious. In a true allegory many points of comparison are made between the surface story and the different story, and it is not always clear what the author intended as an allegorical feature.

It is also possible to make nonallegorical narratives into allegories by applying elements from a different story (existing only in the allegorical interpreter's mind) to aspects of the nonallegorical narrative, under the assumption it is an allegory—as Mark does with the Sower, for example. When this technique is applied to a realistic story and the full allegorical interpretation is set forth, the differences between the two stories are immediately obvious.[4]

While unrestrained allegorical interpretations of Jesus' parables have persisted in confessional religious contexts, few modern scholars familiar with critical methods engage in such allegorical speculation.[5] Many, however, do engage in a kind of "restrained" allegory,[6] but few have set out a deliberate theoretical argument in defense of the allegorical method.[7] One modern scholar who has done so is Craig L. Blomberg.[8]

BLOMBERG'S ALLEGORY

Blomberg clearly recognizes the drawbacks to an unrestrained allegorical interpretation,[9] but argues that a rejection of excessive allegorizing does not invalidate a limited and sober allegorizing of a parable.[10] He begins with the assumption that Jesus was an allegorist, arguing that "by accepting the *possibility* [italics mine] that Jesus himself employed allegory," the critic then has no real need to divide "the parables into authentic and inauthentic bits and pieces," as modern biblical scholarship has done.[11] In fact, the presence of allegorical features in some parables becomes for Blomberg a major criterion for the authenticity of such parables.[12]

Blomberg's major reason for thinking Jesus used allegory is derived from Mark's parables theory (4:11–12), a theory that both Mark and Blomberg trace to the historical Jesus; Blomberg also cites numerous allegorical elements in the parables of Jesus, which he thinks also derive from Jesus.[13] He makes the point that allegory is a common literary convention in Old Testament and rabbinic literature. The many similarities between rabbinic parables and Jesus' parables also help convince Blomberg that Jesus' parables are allegories. Jesus' auditors in the first century would have been accustomed to hearing stories in this fashion, and hence would naturally look for allegorical equivalencies in Jesus' stories as well, Blomberg argues.[14] He also thinks that a majority of Jesus' parables "make exactly three main [allegorical] points," though some make only one point, while others make two. His interpretation of the parables showing the suitability of the three-point limitation is the main defense of his thesis; he offers no theoretical rationale as to why it is three points (or one or two), as opposed to four or five, for example.[15]

The main problem with interpreting a narrative allegorically—even one that is clearly designed as allegory—is: How do readers or auditors know precisely what elements inside the narrative deliberately reference certain specific elements outside the narrative? Or put another way, how does the inventor of the allegory control the narrative so the audience, or reader, will make the associations intended by the allegorist? Blomberg responds, arguing that the Old Testament and rabbinic parables use a large number of set, or stock, images. The average person on the street would have been familiar with this stock imagery and would have automatically applied them to Jesus' parables as they did to the rabbis' parables.

The most common of these stock images are as follows: God is represented by a father, king, judge, or shepherd; God's people by a vineyard, vine, or sheep; the devil by an enemy; final judgment by harvest and grape gathering; and the messianic banquet by a feast, or festal clothing.[16] According to Blomberg, Jesus used the same stock images the rabbis used.[17]

The Barren Fig Tree (Luke 13:6–9) as Read by Blomberg

Here is an example of Blomberg's interpretation of the Barren Fig Tree parable using limited allegory.[18] Since the vineyard is a stock metaphor for Israel in Jewish traditions, it is natural, he argues, to take the fig tree in Jesus' story as representing some of the Jews (in Jesus' day), who are also fruitless. Thus, "the fig tree would naturally symbolize the religious leaders of Israel."[19] But the principle of judgment (i.e., on those who do not repent, mentioned in Luke's setting of the parable—Luke 13:3, 5) "obviously applies universally," though Blomberg does not say why this is so. In Jesus' allegory, two points are clear: (1) The threat of imminent judgment hangs over Israel's leaders (i.e., in the fact that the tree may be cut down); and (2) God, who is represented by the farmer, had offered mercy for a short while (represented by the three years and a potential additional year). The "digging and the manuring" may be "insult humor" if the crowd realized Jesus was talking about Israel's leaders, or it may be nothing more than normal horticultural practice. The vinedresser plays no role in Blomberg's allegory, but he does not tell the reader how he knows this is so. The allegory stresses both mercy (the potential extension of one year of life for the fig tree) and judgment (the tree will be cut down if it does not bear fruit). Blomberg summarizes the message of the allegory in this way: "[T]he announcement of judgment becomes a call to turn to God. It is up to each individual in Jesus' audience to determine his or her own response."

Critique

There are three major difficulties with allegorical readings of parables. First, the realism of Jesus' parables works against the multiple one-to-one analogies demanded by allegory. Blomberg clearly realizes this: Realistic fiction leaves the audience in doubt "about just which details are supposed to have a double meaning," he says.[20] So it is in this story. Blomberg has picked the farmer as a God figure, which is an unfortunate analogy, since the narrative, read for itself, casts both the farmer and the vinedresser as flawed characters, neither of whom seem to know nearly enough about farming in general, and the care of fig trees in particular. For example, the owner does not seem to know that the way to get rid of unwanted trees is by uprooting them, not by cutting them down. And exactly why didn't the vintner dig about the tree and manure it in the previous three years if he thought that such treatment was helpful for fig trees?[21]

Second, the identification of referents inside the parable deliberately pointing outside the parable originates in the mind of the allegorical interpreter and not with the narrative itself. Or put another way, the second story is *evoked* in the mind of the allegorical interpreter by an engagement with the narrative, and actually arises from what the allegorist brings to the narrative. In this case, the farmer serves Blomberg as a convenient referential hook on which to hang his second story about God's mercy and judgment, thus turning a story about two flawed farmers into a theological warning. He clearly knows that the process works this way, in spite of the argument that second-century rabbinic parables allegorized such things as fathers, kings, judges, and shepherds.[22]

Third, the polyvalence of the story works against it being theological. Blomberg is clearly bothered by the vintner, and must have toyed with making him a referential hook on which to hang some aspect of his second story. What keeps him from doing so is his own personal orthodox theology.[23] He does not quite know what to do with the digging about the tree and fertilizing it, saying it *could be* "insult humor" but neglecting to tell his readers exactly how the joke might work at the level of his second story. He simply disregards the three years/one year as insignificant to his allegorical second story. Oddly, he bypasses the vineyard, one of the stock images he finds in rabbinic allegory, and invests his allegory in the fig tree. His failure to find an allegorical reference in the vineyard raises the question: How does a reader know not to invest a "stock metaphor" in Jesus' stories with the same value it has in the rabbinic parables? Others who also practice a restrained allegorical interpretation of Jesus' parables do find referential hooks in a number of the elements that Blomberg bypasses.[24]

Allegorical interpretations of parables consume and dispense with the necessity of the original narrative. If Blomberg's second story is truly what is going on in this parable, we no longer need the story, because the story undermines the interpretation.

Metaphor

Allegory and metaphor, as genres, actually function in similar ways.[25] Allegory is a narrative comprised of numerous individual metaphors, which deliberately fit together to create a different story at another level of concern (e.g., in Bunyan's allegorical *Pilgrim's Progress*, a story about one man's problems in life becomes a story about the life experience of all Christians).[26] Thus, a deliberate allegory (not a story read allegorically) has many points of reference outside itself. Multiple referents are necessary to create a different story. Metaphor, on the other hand, describes one known thing under the guise of a similar yet different thing. Allegory and metaphor differ only in the number of referents.

According to the metaphorical approach, Jesus describes the kingdom of God in stories about common peasant life in first-century Palestine. The first scholar to make this association was C. H. Dodd,[27] but the scholar who did most to launch this approach is Robert Funk. His analysis of the parable about the Samaritan (Luke 10:30–35) as metaphor is classic and modeled the method for critical scholarship.[28] Dominic Crossan, however, has done most to popularize the approach.[29] Crossan describes the parables as poetic metaphor "in which participation precedes information so that the function of [poetic] metaphor is to create participation in the metaphor's referent."[30] Thus, the parables of Jesus do not transmit information, as allegory does. Parables, as metaphors, "articulate a referent so new or so alien to consciousness that this referent can only be grasped within the metaphor itself."[31] According to Crossan, the referent, alien to the human consciousness, is the kingdom of God—or, better, the rule of God. The kingdom is not a static place with borders (as people generally conceive of heaven, for example) but is a symbol designating God's act of ruling with no reference to specific location.[32]

According to Crossan, the parables temporize God's rule, that is, parables bring the kingdom near and make it accessible to human beings in earthy stories about common life in first-century Palestine, or as Crossan puts it, the parables "express and they contain the temporality [i.e., related to human time and space] of Jesus' experience of God; they proclaim and they establish the historicity of Jesus' response to the kingdom."[33] In short, the parables conceptualize in story Jesus' experience of God and his rule. So while allegory and metaphor function in similar ways, they are not the same thing at all, according to Crossan. Allegory has numerous referents, and metaphor, a single referent. Allegory instructs by referencing the correct information, and metaphor reveals by bringing the inexpressible into language.[34]

How do such scholars get from earthy stories about common peasant life to the grand idea of God actively ruling in human life? The parables themselves simply do not, in so many words, self-evidently describe anything so ethereal or theological. They are stories about farming, food production, merchandizing, ranching, murder, robbery, investment, domestic activities, and the like. Exactly how, and where, does a story about common life become a story about specific religious values?

First, scholars begin with the assumption that the rule of God was the overarching passion of Jesus life, and that his public career focused on announcing the advent of God's rule.[35] Two bits of affirmative evidence exist for taking the parables as metaphors for the kingdom, namely, the general early Christian view that Jesus spoke in figures, and the fact that many of Jesus' parables are introduced by a comparative frame: "As it is with [whatever is in the parable], so it is with the kingdom of God/heaven" (as Matthew puts it in 13:24, 31, 33, 44, 45, 47). There is good reason, however, to suspect that this introductory frame did not originate with Jesus but rather originated with a second generation of early Christians trying to make sense of Jesus' parables in their postresurrection worshiping communities.[36] There is also reason to think that Mark was the first to associate the kingdom and the parables.[37]

Scholars treating parables as metaphors must *assume* that a parable is, in fact, metaphorical, since metaphors have no distinctive form giving away their figurative character. A metaphor functions by applying language appropriate to one thing, to another analogous thing. Both things are known, and either stated or implied in the metaphor. The metaphor's use of heightened or unusual language may indicate that a comparison is being made. For example, the following poetic stanzas use metaphor. In the first example below, both the figurative and literal terms are stated and equated. In the second, the literal term is implied, the figurative stated, and both are indirectly but clearly equated.

First example

> Life the hound
> Equivocal
> Comes at a bound
> Either to rend me
> Or to befriend me.[38]

In this metaphor "life" is the subject and "hound" is the vehicle for describing life; life is described as if it were a hound. Both are related by apposition.

Second example

In the second example the poet describes a windy day on the porch of a dilapidated house:

> Leaves got up in a coil and hissed
> Blindly struck at my knee and missed.[39]

In this metaphor an unstated snake is the subject and swirling leaves constitute the vehicle. The poet describes a snake as if it were a pile of leaves. Put another way, the characteristics of leaves on a windy day are applied to a snake. The snake is, of course, implied, but there is no mistaking what is going on in the metaphor.

A metaphor *deliberately* points outside itself to the real subject under consideration, but parables contain no clear internal markers that deliberately and unambiguously take the reader outside the story to a particular referent.[40] Without the comparative frames, which are not part of the inner narrative world of the parable, the stories of Jesus would seem to function like all stories do—they draw readers into their plots.

Images of the kingdom can clearly be *evoked* in the mind of a parable reader, but a reader's evoking the kingdom is not the same as the story deliberately referencing the kingdom. In the first instance, the reader brings the kingdom to the story; in the second, the story brings the reader to the kingdom.

The Barren Fig Tree (Luke 13:6–9) as Read by Scott

Here is an example of a metaphorical explanation of the Barren Fig Tree parable by Brandon Scott.[41] This parable has no comparative frame calling for a comparison,[42] but for Scott parables are assumed to be *mashal,* "a short narrative fiction to reference a transcendent symbol."[43] Therefore, Scott treats all parables figuratively regardless of whether or not they have a comparative frame. Unlike Blomberg, Scott studies only the parable; he does not consider the literary setting in Luke any help in understanding the parable in the time of Jesus, some fifty years or so earlier than Luke.[44] He also begins with the assumption that "the fig tree has strong metaphorical and symbolic possibilities,"[45] but does not draw on that correct insight for his reading of the parable. His literary analysis divides the story into two "acts." Luke 13:6–7, the first act, lays out the tree's barrenness. The three years indicate only that the "fig tree is hopelessly infertile." In the second act (Luke 13:8–9), Scott, like Blomberg, bypasses the digging and fertilizing of the tree as significant features for understanding the parable,[46] but unlike Blomberg, he focuses on the missing apodosis in the vintner's final statement to the owner as the essential element leading to a correct reading of the parable.[47] This ellipsis "creates hope" for the tree "on the reader's part"—that is, a mere possibility exists that the tree will be briefly spared. Scott correctly notes that the story has no ending, no third act. What happened after the vintner's request for more time for the tree? Did the owner let it live for another period of time, or did he order it cut down? For Scott the story turns into a parable about God's rule in the omission (the ellipsis in 13:9), that is, on what is not in the parable. Scott asks, "Can the miracle of birth come from a barren fig tree?" But the parable is silent. The situation appears hopeless for the tree, since it is barren. The only glimmer of hope lies in what the parable does not say, and it is there one finds the kingdom:

> In the parable the ellipsis is the kingdom. We keep on manuring. What else is there to do?[48]

By this Scott apparently means that under the rule of God there is always hope.

Critique

Whence comes this sudden reference to the kingdom? The kingdom clearly is not in the parable, since, as Scott says, the kingdom is in an ellipsis—an omission from the parable. Scott evokes the kingdom from what the story does not say. This is the one and only time he refers to the kingdom in discussing this particular parable. Where does the kingdom come from if it is not in the parable? The answer is that Scott *evokes* the kingdom, but he describes the kingdom as though it were in the parable: "The ellipsis is the kingdom." In associating parable and kingdom in this way, he has not drawn a careful enough line between what the parable does say and his own response to it.

On the other hand, his teacher, Robert Funk, in his model of the metaphorical method is careful to document the location of the hermeneutical leap from story to kingdom.[49] He explains the story of the Samaritan (Luke 10:30b–35) *using the language of the story* (as Scott also does, for that matter). For Funk, understanding the story means that an auditor allows himself or herself to be drawn into the story and become like the man in the ditch who is helped by an enemy. "The 'meaning' of the parable is the way auditors take up roles in the story and play out the drama. Response will vary from person to person and from time to time." Putting the story into different language, however, is a particular reader's abstraction of the story, Funk correctly insists. Funk's own final abstraction—his response to the story—is: "[I]n the kingdom mercy is always a surprise."[50] The only time he mentions the kingdom in his discussion is when he abstracts the story; his abstraction is his own personal response to the story.

In his discussion of this parable, Crossan, like Scott, also blurs the line between story and response, and describes the leap from literal (story) to figurative (kingdom) as the story's reference rather than his own personal response:

> [I]f we abandon finally and completely the idea [that the story of the Samaritan is an example story], we must see this as a parable and so suggest the leap from the literal point to the metaphorical point which is the real purpose of the literary creation. The literal point confronted the hearers with the necessity of saying the impossible and having their world turned upside down. . . . The metaphorical point is that *just so* does the kingdom of God break abruptly into human consciousness.[51]

Thus, it becomes incumbent upon readers to quantify precisely what in each story leads a reader to a particular abstraction of the narrative. In this way critics can evaluate whether it is the narrative that unambiguously leads the reader's mind away from the story in a particular direction, or whether it is the reader's own imagination that leads to a particular abstraction of the story in different language.

SYMBOL

So far as I know, no one has actually argued that the parables of Jesus are symbols. Symbol was introduced into parables discussion by Norman Perrin, who argued successfully that the "kingdom of God" was itself a symbol: "Kingdom of God is a symbol which evokes the myth of the activity of God as king on behalf of his people," and because it was symbol "this activity of God could be understood in different ways."[52] He still affirmed, however, that the parables of Jesus functioned as metaphors, which referenced a symbol—the kingdom of God.[53]

Symbol is related to allegory, simile, similitude, and metaphor, but is distinct from them. Simply stated, a symbol is what it is, and something more besides, but the "something more" cannot be precisely quantified.[54] "The symbol is the richest and at the same time the most difficult of the poetical figures. Both its richness and its difficulty result from its imprecision. . . . It is like an opal that flashes out different colors when slowly turned in the light."[55] The symbol signifies something beyond itself, or has a range of reference beyond itself. In the case of public symbols shared in a given community, the "something more" may be, more or less, clear, because all in the community share a general understanding of the symbol to some extent. But in the case of private symbols, evoked and used by individual writers and unique to each writer, the "something more" may be almost impossible to identify with precision.[56]

To judge from the wide range of responses to the parables in biblical scholarship, parables seem to function more like private symbols than metaphors and allegories. Clearly, parables have evoked for biblical scholars a broad range of references, and to judge from the diversity of meanings they find in the parables, the "something more besides" has no particular specificity. That is to say, the symbol does not deliberately reference *one* particular thing more. The parabolic symbol (if such it is) is not a cipher that stands for some other particular thing; rather, the symbol evokes responses by suggesting something more beyond itself, and readers/auditors fill in the substance of the symbol as they will. In the sense that a symbol embodies the idea or quality it evokes, a symbol at the level of literal language may be said "to partake of the reality which it renders intelligible."[57] Crossan sees that same association between the metaphor and its referent, and puts it this way in his discussion of the parable of the Samaritan: "The hearer struggling with the contradictory dualism of Good/Samaritan is actually experiencing in and through this the inbreaking of the Kingdom. Not only does it happen like this, it happens in this."[58] James M. Robinson expresses the same sentiment about parables in general: Parables are "God's advent in language."[59] If parables are symbols, their "meaning" is what the symbol evokes for a particular reader, and is a reader's response. Symbols do not reference as metaphor does, so the symbolic "something more" is what the reader determines it is.

Some first-century Jews may well have taken the Barren Fig Tree parable as a story symbolizing Israel as God's special people (and related ideas—symbols are not precise). Fig trees are used in the Hebrew Bible as symbols for both the blessing and judgment of God.[60] The fig tree may languish at times because of God's judgment (Joel 1:12), and may even be cut down, as this story suggests, but God does not abandon his people. Like trees that are cut down and flourish again (Job 14:7–9), if Israel is brought low, she will nevertheless flourish once more (Isa 11:1, 10), for God cannot reject or deny his own. This is the same conclusion reached by the Jewish-Christian writer Paul, who also used tree imagery (Rom 11). In Luke's story about the fig tree, no decision about the tree has been made, but even if it is cut down, clearly a shoot will spring up from the stump, for that is the way of trees. Israel as the chosen people of God is the parent symbol that incorporates the related ideas of blessing and judgment.

I hasten to add that this "reading" in the previous paragraph is not in the story or even referenced by the story. Rather, it is my personal hypothetical reconstruction of an understanding I imagine could have been possible for some first-century Jews. Israel as the people of God, fig trees communicating judgment and blessing, and the survival of the people constitute the "something more" of symbolism, which some first-century auditors may have found in the story.

8

Jesus the Ethicist

Parable as Moral Lesson and Codification for Social Reform

The two scholars whose methods are discussed in this chapter are widely separated in time. Adolf Jülicher, who regarded parables as figurative speech expressing a single idea, wrote near the end of the nineteenth century. William R. Herzog II, who regards parables as constructs encouraging social reform, wrote a major work on parables near the end of the twentieth century. While separated both temporally and methodologically, they do share the similar idea that Jesus' parables related to moral behavior in society.

PARABLES AS MORAL LESSONS: ADOLF JÜLICHER

Jülicher could have been discussed in the previous chapter, since he holds that parables are figurative speech, but his emphasis on the general moral character of the ideas he finds in the parables also associates him with the work of Herzog, for whom the parables are a type of social analysis intended to empower peasant reform in the first century.[1] I have chosen to discuss Jülicher's view in connection with Herzog because Jülicher's interpretation of the parables treats Jesus as "a teacher of wisdom who inculcated moral precepts and a simplified theology" by means of his parables.[2]

Jülicher began his study of parables with an extensive survey of what he termed "scientific studies" of the parables, beginning with the apostolic fathers (second century) and reaching to his own day.[3] He concluded that the survey demonstrated his thesis: In spite of hundreds of years of ecclesiastical allegorizing of the parables, the parables continue to give the impression of naturalness and realism.[4] The strange allegorical ideas brought to Jesus' words through the centuries have been unable to shake that impression. As long as one does not begin with the allegorical interpretations of the parables, a clear distinction exists between what Jesus said in parables and the ideas brought to his words by his interpreters.[5] This distinction, Jülicher argued, is the final proof that allegory, with its multiple meanings, is a bankrupt method for reading parables. Jülicher said that "simplicity is the sign of truth" (*simplex sigillum veri*),[6] meaning that simple explanations have a clear ring of authenticity. Critical scholarship has, in the main, continued to agree with his conclusion that the parables of Jesus are not allegories,[7] and his book brought about fundamental changes in the way parables were studied in critical scholarship, though, to be sure, the allegorical method persists in modern scholarship even today.[8]

Drawing on distinctions made by Aristotle, Jülicher argued that allegory and parable are essentially two different literary types. As comparison (*Vergleichung* = simile) is basic to the parable, so metaphor is basic to allegory.[9] Allegory is actually expanded metaphor, as simile is expanded into similitude (*Gleichnis*).[10] Jülicher found that the genre "parable" was comprised of three types. The first, *Gleichnis* (similitude), is a briefly expanded comparison (i.e., simile). He called the second type *Fabel* (fable, or story parable); this type, comprised of similitudes extended into narrative, constitutes what we know as the narrative parables of Jesus.[11] The third type, of which there are only four in the New Testament, is the *Beispielerzählung* (example story).[12]

All three classes of parable function in the same way—their fundamental element is simple comparison. In a comparison, two concepts are set side by side to illustrate similarity. Between the two lies a third element, a single point, relating the one to the other. Basically, parables work like similes, that is, by comparison. They have two parts: a picture half (i.e., the narrative image in the parable), and a substance half (i.e., the real matter at issue in the image).[13] The third part, joining them together, is the point of comparison. Think of the parable as a brief narrative image evoking a general moral; that moral is the real matter at issue in the image. The picture half is drawn from things familiar to first-century audiences and therefore really did not need explanation. These images of first-century life were intended to facilitate an understanding of the real matter, which is the moral. By staying focused on the parable and not getting lost in the details, as allegorical interpreters do, something could be learned from the image half, and applied to the real matter at issue.[14]

In the similitude and story parable, the substantial issue is not stated in so many words, and must be drawn from the image by extrapolating one central point, idea, or major theme of the widest generality.[15] For example, Jülicher regarded the story of the Samaritan (Luke 10:30–35) as a narrative that "illustrates an idea of universal validity in the form of a particular incident."[16] In the example story, the two halves come together, the parable providing a particular example of the universal truth it was intended to illustrate. The Samaritan, for example, illustrates the general principle of compassionate self-sacrifice.[17]

The Barren Fig Tree (Luke 13:6–9) as Read by Jülicher

Jülicher begins with a careful analysis of the parable as a realistic story, in order to show its naturalness.[18] The fig tree is the main focus of the story. Because it is deliberately planted in the vineyard, it must be construed as a valuable part of the property. The natural assumption is that the current owner planted it, but that is not clear from the narrative. Its presence in the vineyard is not unexpected or unusual, since fig trees in vineyards are a natural occurrence in the Orient. The vintner is the owner's slave, charged with the tending of the vineyard.

The owner has come looking for figs on this tree for three years; his current trip comes during the fourth year that the tree has not borne figs. The owner decides on a radical solution to the problem of a fig tree now fruitless for four years: Cut the tree down; it is needlessly occupying space in the vineyard and draining off the resources of the land. The vintner petitions the owner for another year, requesting that he be allowed to dig about it and manure it. Such treatment is natural and actually should have been done once each year in the previous years as a part of the tree's normal care. Therefore, since the vintner suggests doing what must be considered normal care, it is clear that the vintner had not provided such care for the tree in the previous three years. Had he done so, he would have known that normal care would scarcely be effective in the fourth year. What the tree really needs, at this point, is extraordinary care.

The vintner's statement to the owner, "you shall cut it down," is an inappropriate way for a slave to address his master, and likely should be read as an indirect future: "it shall be cut down." The narrative is not resolved at the end. Is the tree cut down or does it have an extended year of existence? The narrator has no particular interest in resolving the conundrum of Luke 13:9. In sum, the parable is a vivid image of a tree whose destruction is absolutely certain if it does not take advantage of its new opportunity and produce fruit.

"The context [in Luke] shows what the story should teach," Jülicher says.[19] Luke 13:1–9 forms a narrative unit, with the connection between parable and context coming in the similarity between 13:3, 5, and 13:9: The parable supports the two warnings in 13:3, 5, and the two warnings make the point of the parable clear. Just as an unfruitful fig tree will be destroyed if it does not take advantage of its second chance (13:9), so "all of you" (13:3, 5) who ignore the allotted time for repentance will perish. In this way, Jesus requires his audience to move from the image (*Bild*) to the real matter (*Sache*) at issue in the parable, to make the leap from judgment on an unfruitful fig tree to an appropriate application in a completely different sphere. Under similar conditions, people in the completely different sphere will perish just like the fig tree. But if they take advantage of the opportunity for repentance, their deserved punishment will be stayed.

The general religious truth of this parable for Jülicher is that all who will not repent will perish. The "moral" is best expressed in Rom 2:3–4: "Do you presume upon the riches of his kindness and forbearance and patience? Do you not know that God's kindness is meant to lead you to repentance?" (2:4 RSV). For Jülicher, this parable also has a more specific historical application. As Luke shows (13:1–5), Jesus is speaking this parable to his people, Israel. "The horrible fate of a few pious Jews provided a good occasion for a people weighted down in spiritual pride and certainty to be presented with their own horoscope (13:3, 5), and to have it illustrated in a parable: The Israel of Jesus' day finds itself in the situation of the fig tree in its year of grace secured by the gardener."[20] Nevertheless, the fig tree does not exactly represent Israel. One can make the association, however, because in that context the parable acquires "its deepest and richest sense."[21]

Critique

The leap from image to moral occurs in Jülicher's mind under the influence of Luke's literary setting (13:1–5). The setting may actually be how Luke understood the parable, since it immediately precedes the parable and most interpreters do read the parable under the influence of Luke's setting.[22] Jülicher's explanation of the way the parable is introduced ("and he was speaking this parable," 13:6; cf. 21:29; 4:24; 11:5; 15:11), however, may have been a more significant break than Jülicher allowed. If so, Luke could have associated the parable with what followed, and, that being the case, Luke may have seen something in the parable other than repentance.[23] The shift in language from "if it bears fruit next year" and "cut it down," to "repentance" and "you will perish" is a great leap, for it brings to the story a theological dimension that is not part of the story about a farming problem. In its own way, Jülicher's treatment of the parable is not unlike what he accused the allegorists of doing. In the final analysis, Jülicher's general moral about repentance relating the image to the real matter is simply another reader's response to the narrative.

Jülicher has been criticized for his formulation of general morals he finds as the point of the parables; they turn out to be morals more at home in late-nineteenth-century liberal German Protestantism than in first-century Judaism.[24] Thus, they are scarcely apt to be the way first-century Jews could have responded to the parables. One reviewer has referred to them as "often slack epigrams lacking eschatological glory."[25]

Others have criticized Jülicher's idea that the parables were essentially instructional in nature, that is, that parables were designed to teach a moral of some sort. This idea came to Jülicher through Aristotle from the educational system of classical antiquity. Jesus lived in a very different environment, in the context of ancient Judaism with its own way of transmitting traditions. Jülicher's principle mistake, his critics say, was to place Jesus in an ancient Greek schoolroom rather than in the context of ancient Judaism. Perrin sums it up this way: "Aristotle's categories were ultimately to be found inappropriate to an understanding of the parables of Jesus."[26] A bigger problem is that Jülicher tried to collapse the many things going on in the parable into one single point. It is, in a sense, an attempt to reduce the polyvalence of the parable, which even the least sophisticated reader can see clearly enough.

One major problem with Jülicher's explanation of this particular parable is that his moral point hinges on an assumption the story specifically disallows. In spite of his careful analysis of the realism of the narrative, Jülicher nevertheless assumes that the fig tree will have another year of grace for bearing fruit. Jülicher himself even notes that, in the end, the parable simply fails to resolve the future of the fig tree. Nevertheless, his interpretation still assumes that the tree will have a future opportunity for fruit bearing, just as the people in Luke 13:1–5 are given opportunity to repent. The story leaves readers uncertain as to the fate of the fig tree. There is simply no indication how the owner responded to the vintner's request to leave the tree for another year.[27] Thus, Jülicher's point of comparison, which brings context and parable together in the interpretation, is not to be found in the parable.

PARABLE AS CODIFICATION FOR SOCIAL REFORM: WILLIAM HERZOG II

Herzog's unique perspective on parables began with his inability to arrive at a satisfactory theological conclusion for the parable of the Laborers in the Vineyard (Matt 20:1–16). The vineyard owner simply could not be a disguised God figure who acted graciously, as the usual interpretations would have it.[28] His failure to find a satisfactory theological resolution to the parable led him to inquire into its social scientific background and to make a closer examination of the socioeconomic context of first-century Palestine, or as he put it:

> The task of understanding the end of that parable turned out to be no simple matter. . . . It required knowing who appeared in the parable, where they fit into the configuration of their society, what roles they were playing, what classes or social groups they represented, how land owners and day laborers were related to each other socially and economically, why the workers were standing in the agora all day, why they were hired to work in a vineyard, why they were hired for only one day and paid at the end of the day, why some were hired for less than a day and how much they could have expected to be paid, how much a denarius was worth in their social setting, why the owner paid them in reverse order, and why they were offended at the owner's generosity.[29]

These socioeconomic questions led him to unique conclusions about the nature of parables. They are not allegories, metaphors, or stories with a one-point moral. They are not harmless stories that teach theology and benign morals. Rather, they are "earthy stories with heavy meanings," addressing the exploitation of a peasant class. They present in narrative the "gory details of how oppression served the interests of a ruling class." And "they explored how human beings could break the spiral of violence and cycle of poverty created by exploitation and oppression."[30] Thus, the parables for Herzog are a kind of social analysis by Jesus, in which he represented "typifications of everyday life." In short, parables are brief narrative constructs accurately portraying social conditions in Palestinian society.[31]

But why would Jesus create such stories about peasant life in first-century Palestine and tell them to peasants? The answer to that question for Herzog lay in finding some larger strategy in terms of which the Jesus of the parables could be explained as a subversive figure whose threat to the ruling powers (the Romans) resulted in his death.[32] A Jesus who taught spiritual mastery of the inner person through a private relationship with God would scarcely have been controversial for the secular authorities. Indeed, he would likely have been welcomed, and even "supported by the Romans as part of their rural pacification program" of the peasant population.[33] A Jesus who "dispensed heavenly truths through literary gems called parables" would not "have been executed as a political subversive and crucified between two social bandits on the charge of subversion."[34]

Herzog finds a rationale for the "larger strategy" in the work of Paulo Freire, a twentieth-century educator and Marxist, whose work with literacy programs in Brazil brought about his imprisonment and eventual exile from Brazil. Later Freire moved to Chile, where he continued his work, and eventually to a position with the World Council of Churches.[35] Freire reasoned that the education peasants received from the government was "banking education"—instruction intended to convince "the oppressed [i.e., the peasants] either that change is impossible or that any challenge to the existing order is a diabolical assault on a divinely preordained world."[36] In other words, banking education was an investment in maintaining the status quo. In this way, an elite ruling class maintained and extended control over an oppressed disfranchised peasant class. Freire, on the other hand, invested his energies in what he called a "problem-posing education," an educational program designed "to remake and reform the world."[37]

To teach peasants to read, Freire and his teams listened to village conversation. From this, Freire "developed a vocabulary out of the daily language of the illiterates themselves,"[38] reduced these "generative" words to a visual image, and presented the image to a "culture circle" of peasants for discussion. The generative words were the basis of the peasant language, which expressed their view of the world, "and yielded a culture no less important than the high culture of the elites."[39] This process made it possible for peasants to objectify and analyze their own culture.[40] Learning to read in this fashion enabled the peasants also to read their society, so as to see it in terms of problems to be solved (what Freire calls "decoding"). "The very act of converting a final fact or unquestioned truth into a problem reveals the world as a human construction susceptible to change and . . . exposes the oppressors' [i.e., the elite class] efforts to present the world as a divinely sanctioned order."[41] The process of coding (generative words into images), analyzing, and decoding leads peasants to "conscientization," an awareness (Herzog calls it "a process akin to experiencing revelation")[42] leading to "reflection and action upon the world in order to transform it."[43] Thus, "the oppressed become subjects capable of making history by remaking their society. They accept their vocation as historical subjects and they become agents of humanization in a dehumanizing society."[44]

Herzog recognizes that there are differences between Jesus and Freire, not the least of which is the time frame that separates them.[45] But there are also similarities: Both Jesus and Freire worked with the poor, oppressed, and peasants; both lived in similar social contexts (advanced agrarian societies); both worked in similar societies (from the standpoint of the sociology of the area); both worked in societies "deformed by colonial exploitation"; religion played an important role in the lives of rural peasants of both their worlds; and both were teachers with similar students, namely, the illiterate, the marginalized, and the poor.[46] Jesus lived in an agrarian society,[47] and in that context his parables functioned much like Freire's "problem-posing education." According to Herzog, Jesus' parables "re-present a familiar or typified scene for the purpose of generating conversation about and stimulating the kinds of reflection that expose contradictions in popularly held beliefs or traditional thinking."[48]

Why did Jesus do this? What was the object of the parable? According to Herzog, the parable encodes "the systems of oppression that controlled their [peasant] lives and held them in bondage. . . . The parable . . . was a codification designed to stimulate social analysis and to expose the contradictions between the actual situation of its hearers and the Torah of God's justice."[49] Jesus' parables, therefore, could conceivably have led to social unrest—or even, perhaps, to revolt—since they dealt with political and economic issues. In this way, Herzog provides a plausible historical rationale for the crucifixion of Jesus, a nagging problem for those who ponder parables. Why would anyone want to kill someone who told such charming stories?[50] Herzog provides an answer: He was a political threat to the state because he empowered the peasants.[51]

The Laborers in the Vineyard (Matt 20:1–16) as Read by Herzog

Herzog signals the way he reads the parable by the title of his chapter: "Blaming the Victims of Oppression."[52] In his view, the narrative deals with a problem in labor management from the perspective of the elite class—"the ideologies used to blame the victim and to keep day laborers separated and paralyzed by self-hatred."[53] He rejects Matthew's contextualizing of the parable. Matthew provides an introductory comparative frame (20:1a) and a concluding interpretation (20:16) in order to imbue the narrative with theological values.[54] Matthew has misled every interpreter into seeing the vineyard owner as a God figure. The problem of the parable's interpretation through the years has been the following: how to "justify the owner's concluding words [20:14–15] and vilify the workers" (i.e., to make them the villains in the story), so as to secure an adequate theological interpretation consistent with the vineyard owner being a God figure. To this end, all "interpreters ignored the workers' voices so that the action of the owner could be construed as an example of God's gracious, generous goodness."[55]

Herzog treats the canonical version of the parable (20:1b–15). Hence, Matt 20:15 is the conclusion.[56] The vineyard owner is part of an elite class (a patron), since he has a steward and owns a vineyard producing such an immense harvest that he is unable to calculate exactly how many workers are needed.[57] High unemployment exists in the area, for the agora is filled with workers at all hours of the day. The owner takes advantage of these unemployed workers in order to meet the needs of his harvest by offering them work without a wage agreement (20:4–6).[58] When it comes time to pay the workers, the owner gives the steward specific instructions about paying the workers and hangs around to observe; normally the steward would handle this task alone. By having the owner hire the laborers and hang around to observe their pay at the end of the day, Jesus is "codifying" (making visible) to peasants their own oppression.

Thus, the parable is designed to depict "a confrontation between two social classes who might never have encountered each another"—the owner and a peasant workman.[59]

The wage each is paid, a denarius for the day's work, is scarcely generous; in fact, it is not even a subsistence wage because day laborers did not work every day.[60] In what appears to be a depressed labor market (more workers than jobs available), the elite owner offers, at best, a subsistence wage to the first workers hired (20:2), and the other workers "are so desperate that they go to the vineyard [without an agreement], hoping to receive some portion of a denarius" for their partial day's work (20:3–7).[61]

The owner instructs the steward to deviate from the normal order for paying workers (first hired are normally the first paid) by paying the last hired first, in order deliberately to insult the first workers hired. By paying the workers hired first at the end of the pay line, and paying them the same as the later workers hired, the owner shows that "he values their daylong effort . . . no more than the brief labor of the eleventh-hour workers." They quite rightly take this as an insult (20:12), and protest.[62] The elite owner then picks out their leader and makes an example of him (20:13). The term "friend" in the context of a conversation between an elite vineyard owner and an expendable day laborer is scarcely a genuine friendly remark; the distance between the two classes is too great for that to be even a remote possibility. "It is condescending and subtly reinforces their different social stations, yet it feigns courtesy."[63] The owner's dismissal of this man ("Take what belongs to you and go," 20:14) is a banishment of the worker, effectively blackballing him from further employment. The dismissal is intended to intimidate the other workers, whom the owner, in the end, blames for the problem: Did you not agree with me for the usual daily wage? (20:13)—a statement "cloaked, like all victim blaming, in apparent courtesy and concern."[64]

Critique

In general, reviewers have been positive about Herzog's insights into the economic features of the parables.[65] There are difficulties, however. While virtually no one denies that Herzog has recognized a neglected element in certain of Jesus' parables,[66] the idea that all of Jesus' parables were deliberately designed to lead to a social analysis geared to expose the unjust conditions of a peasant class is less clear. For example, the nature parables of Jesus are not as amenable to Herzog's economic approach. (The only parables that do not treat human activity in some fashion are a Mustard Seed, a Sprouting Seed, the Ear of Grain, the Date Palm Shoot—even a Sower is virtually a nature story.)[67] And some of the other parables dealing with individual human action or society do not, on the surface at least, appear to raise the issue of social justice and the economic imbalance between elites and expendable peasants in the first century.[68] It would be a stretch to accommodate such parables under Herzog's theory of parables. A theory explaining how the parables of Jesus work must accommodate all the parables in order to be completely convincing. This statement, however, does not deny the novel features Herzog has recognized in some of the parables.

One reviewer has faulted Herzog for his use of a "macrosociological" model for explaining the agrarian society of first-century Palestine "rather than a comparative anthropological or traditional historical approach." The model of Palestinian culture Herzog uses is a modern construct, and the reviewer argues that it is likely faulty. Herzog's choice to use it, the reviewer says, "is a fateful one, for in choices between what the model says 'must be' and what history suggests 'was the case,' H[erzog] will choose the model."[69]

According to Herzog, the parables of Jesus do not teach specific morals or theological truths; they are essentially nonreferential constructs. Jesus designed them as representations of conditions typical of first-century peasant life to describe the inequities of an oppressive economic system. By confronting peasants with their economic bondage through these "typifications," Jesus intended to sensitize them to the inequities of the system to the end that they reform it—in other words, that they seek social justice for themselves. Thus, Jesus becomes a first-century social reformer.

Aspects of Herzog's theory clearly seem correct: The parables are typifications of first-century life (accepted by virtually all parables scholars). They are not referential (accepted by only a very few). Parables are not didactic stories intended to teach a particular "truth" (accepted by only a very few). Parables should be read against the social scientific background of the first century (accepted by most). Parables aim to engage the auditor and solicit a response (accepted by many). Some of the parables clearly address economic and social issues, and reflect a strong interest in social justice (Herzog has clearly made a convincing case). On the other hand, the idea that Jesus should be understood *simply* as a social reformer may go too far; the parables reflect concerns and issues more complex than Herzog's theory can accommodate.[70]

Herzog treats the parables from the perspective that the parable apparently controls the response of auditors.[71] For Herzog, parables are, after all, a means of empowering the peasant population for reforming the social order. Here the theory founders, since, as Herzog himself seems to realize,[72] it is simply not possible to control how any auditor will respond.[73] In the final analysis, Herzog's response to the parables is one more "reader's response." Even though Herzog clearly does provide valuable new insights into some of the parables, he has not provided the ultimate theoretical key to the parables of Jesus.

9

Jesus the Existentialist and Bard

Parable as Existential Narrative and Poetic Fiction

A gap of about thirty years separates the two scholars discussed in this chapter, but they are nonetheless closely related. Dan Otto Via Jr. published his seminal study of the parables of Jesus in 1967, and drawing heavily on Via's insights into the literary character of the parables, I published mine in 1994.

PARABLES AS EXISTENTIAL NARRATIVES: DAN OTTO VIA JR.

Via's book signals a major shift in the study of parables. Until Via, parables had only been regarded as figures of some sort—allegorical, metaphorical, or images portraying a brief moral. Via, on the other hand, argued that parables are "freely invented stories."[1] They are, in short, narrative fictions, and, as such, share the characteristics of, and function like, any narrative does. Like any novel, parables have plots, characters, and action, and they may be analyzed as any piece of narrative literature is analyzed.[2] As invented fictions, parables are literary art, like poems, novels, statuary, paintings, or plays are art. Thus parables, like other forms of art, can be appreciated for their aesthetics—their beauty. As one can appreciate a painting by Monet without knowing either the history of art or the artist's life, so one can appreciate the parables as literary art without knowing anything about Jesus. Like Monet's paintings, they are independent and autonomous, and may be appreciated for what they are in themselves.[3] Thus, Via calls them "aesthetic objects."

Here is the way he reasons about parables as aesthetic objects. The many elements in a narrative relate first of all to each other within the narrative to comprise the whole that the parable is. The elements of the parable are centripetal. Thus, the narrative's organic structure is not dictated by events or ideas outside of the narrative; rather, the narrative whole is determined by its own inner creative organization.[4]

The peculiar function of language used aesthetically is that through its centripetal interlocking of content into form it grasps the attention of the beholder as a total psychosomatic unity—including conscious and unconscious aspects—in an intransitive or nonreferential way.[5] Because it can attract attention to itself in a nonreferential way (i.e., attract attention to itself as an object of interest), the artistic literary creation is, therefore, autonomous, having an existence independent from its creator's intentions. True, it may have connections to the creator's life, "but these are of no critical importance, because they are fused into the new configuration" of the work in the process of its creation.[6]

Works of literary art reveal something that cannot be traced to the author's biography or environment. The author's intention "is neither available nor desirable as a standard for judging the success" of the work. The only important consideration is the internal meaning of the work itself.[7]

Via accepts two canons of literary criticism, which influence his thinking about the autonomy of "aesthetic language": the affective fallacy and the intentional fallacy.[8] The intentional fallacy rules out measuring the artistic work against the standard of what the author intended, because what is obviously important about the work is what it is—that is, what the author actually accomplished, not what he or she intended. The affective fallacy, on the other hand, rules out making the work's affect on the reader the standard for measuring the work. In short, the norm of the work is the work itself. In this sense the work stands on its own over against what the author intended and what critics may think of it.

As applied to the parables, calling them aesthetic objects means that whatever Jesus may have intended with his parables, in the final analysis, is not really accessible to a modern scholar or reader. Since he is not here, no one can ask him about his intentions. Furthermore, what he *intended* is unimportant, since we have ready at hand what he actually *accomplished*—and it speaks for itself.[9]

What then is the "payoff" for studying the parables of Jesus? What do we get from them if we cannot know what Jesus intended with them? Scholars who seek a historical meaning of the parables—what Via calls a "severely historical approach"—ignore the basic human element in the parables (i.e., their "existential" element). Via argues that we should not interpret the parables by the circumstances of Jesus' life; rather, we should interpret Jesus' situation by means of the parables.[10] The parables do not give us information about Jesus' situation and life, but rather they provide readers "an understanding of the possibilities of existence which his situation brought."[11] What Via means by "existence" is this: human beings "in historical encounters in the world, man as an essentially linguistic being using his language to understand his place in history."[12] The parables communicate something about the nature of human existence—that is, human beings as human beings in the world. But parables go beyond simply describing particular human beings in a particular historical situation at a particular time. Via cites Bornkamm's evaluation of the parables as having a broad universal "human" appeal, not just an appeal to particular first-century Jewish human beings: The parable is essentially a question

> aimed straight at the hearer himself, which neither demands from him knowledge, or theoretical judgment, nor presupposes his goodness or education. The only presumption which is made in Jesus' parables is man, the hearer himself, man indeed in the plain, unadorned reality of his world, which is neither put to rights according to high moral standards, nor deplored with righteous indignation.[13]

For Via, the parables dramatize how Jesus understood human existence (i.e., human beings in historical encounters). What is translatable from the parables at the end of the day are ways of understanding how to be human. Thus, a parable brings into language particular ways of being human, and dramatizes certain possibilities of human existence open to everyone, not just first-century human beings. These possibilities, portrayed in the parable, are both positive and negative. Via calls them authentic and inauthentic existence. Thus, the parables portray human beings in their historical encounters in the world as either gaining existence (authentic existence) or losing existence (inauthentic existence). The parables dramatize how such gain or loss occurs. For example, he says the prodigal son gains his existence at the end of the narrative, while the unforgiving servant loses his.[14]

The Laborers in the Vineyard (Matt 20:1–16) as Read by Via

Literary criticism finds two basic plot types to narrative in Western literature: comedy and tragedy. Since the parables are aesthetic narrative (like fiction), Via examines the parables according to their plot type and concludes that "these two basic plot structures are clearly seen in [the parables in] a number of cases."[15] He discusses selected parables under these two plot types.[16] The comic parables have plots that move upward "toward well-being and the inclusion of the protagonist in a new or renewed society." In the tragic parables the plot falls away "toward catastrophe and the isolation of the protagonist from society."[17] The protagonist is the principal character of the parable,[18] and the plot types are essentially describing positive or negative outcomes for the main character in the parable.

For Via, the vineyard owner is the main character of the parable of the Laborers in the Vineyard,[19] and the narrative has a comic plot.[20] For two reasons, he regards Matt 20:16 as Matthew's interpretation of the narrative: The same statement appears in three other contexts (Matt 19:30; Mark 10:31; Luke 13:30), and the reversal motif "does not really get at the meaning of the parable."[21] He does not discuss the introductory comparative frame in Matt 20:1—"For the kingdom of heaven is like"—but it plays no part in his interpretation of the parable. The sequence in which the workers are paid (20:8b), however, is essential to the narrative. In order to achieve the dissatisfaction of the first workers hired, they have to see the workers hired later being paid.[22]

Although the story is about the vineyard owner, there is a "sense in which this parable is the story of the grumbling, full-day workers"—an emphasis most interpreters have missed.[23] Their irritation over being paid the same as the workers who were hired later in the day "gives the parable its formal shape."[24]

The situation in the parable is set up by the vineyard owner hiring workers for the vineyard at various times of the day. Some kind of urgency is suggested by the fact that he must go several times in the day to hire workers (but Via does not elaborate on this feature). The claim of the idle workers in the marketplace that they could not get work "may or may not have been sincere."[25] In order that the surprise at the end of the narrative might not be spoiled, the vineyard owner does not tell the workers hired late in the day what they will be paid.

The middle of the parable describes the workers hired later being paid first, thus prompting the complaint of the workers hired first (20:12). This action sets up the conclusion where the vineyard owner dismisses the complaining workers (20:14–15). Via concludes that the parable has "an interlocking plot moving downward from the well-being of the full-day workers to their exclusion from the presence of a good man."[26]

Clearly there is tragedy in this parable, Via avers, for the workers hired first in the end find themselves estranged "from a gracious benefactor."[27] Via acknowledges that from the standpoint of plot, the parable should likely have been discussed as a tragic parable, but he includes it among his discussion of comic parables because the parable has comic features as well: The exclusion of the workers hired first "is not as emphatic" as other tragic parables, and the narrative emphasizes the goodness of the vineyard owner, from whose generosity the last hired workers benefit at the end. "From the thematic standpoint," these comic features are enough to reverse the story's downward spiral into an upward movement.

Via explains that all narratives have plot and theme. These are closely related: Plot is the theme of the narrative "in movement" (i.e., the dramatic action of the narrative) and theme is the plot "at a standstill" (which Via summarizes as "the point" of the narrative).[28] Literary critics, however, describe theme simply as "a central or dominating idea in a work."[29] The theme, or central idea, of this parable, according to Via, is the vineyard owner's generosity, a clear comic feature.[30]

The grumbling workers—those hired first—insisted on a merit system; they wanted to be paid on the basis of what each worker accomplished. The workers hired last should not have been paid as much as they (the workers hired first) were paid, they argue, because those hired last did not work as long. To Via, this signifies that the workers hired first were secure in their own abilities. Compensation on the basis of generosity, however, threw "an incalculable element [into] human relationships" and seriously challenged their "sense of being able to provide for [their] own security."[31] The workers hired first wanted to be responsible for their own security, and that is why they saw the vineyard owner as unfair and "the incalculable, not as graciousness but as injustice."[32] In the final analysis, they excluded themselves from the generosity of the owner "because of their impenetrable legalistic understanding of existence, grounded in the effort to effect their own security."[33]

The surprising element in the parable is that some workers are paid a full day's wage for one hour of work. This suggests to us again, Via argues, that the divine dimension may cross our everyday reality to produce a crisis of ultimate importance in the midst of the ordinary. Our very existence depends on whether we will accept God's gracious dealings, which shatter our calculations about how things ought to be ordered in the world.[34]

God's graciousness, Via argues, extends to human beings an opportunity to exist meaningfully in the world apart from human merit, but many "may be too calculating to accept the risks" of relying only on God's grace. The tragedy is that they lose their existence.[35] For Via, existing authentically in the world means "existence in faith." Inauthentic existence is "existence in unfaith"[36]—trying to secure your own existence apart from the grace of God—or in the language of the parable, "These last worked only one hour, and you have made them equal to us who have borne the burden of the day and the scorching heat" (20:12 RSV).

Critique

Via's theory of the parables, what they are and how they work, is different from every theory that preceded him, and his reviewers noted the uniqueness of his approach. One reviewer titled his review article "Biblical Scholarship in a New Vein," and described Via's approach as "both refreshing and effective."[37] His book was heralded as a possible "harbinger of things to come,"[38] "a significant first move in what may become a major rescue operation," which aims "to deliver the Christian faith from myth."[39] "Via's literary-critical discussion of the parables is of real interest and obvious importance."[40] Nevertheless in spite of the positive reviews, parables interpretation over the last twenty-five years has continued to be practiced in a "business as usual" mode.[41] For the most part, Via's literary-critical insights suffer benign neglect.

There were also criticisms. One critic "was struck by the commonplace nature of many of Via's interpretations. . . . There has to be more to the parables than that!"[42] The same reviewer continues, that likely Via's interpretations suffer from failure to pay enough attention to "the dynamic interaction between text and interpreter." The parabolic language still has life; thus, the interpreter's task is not "to dissect it for the sake of its translatable content."[43] Another reviewer noted that his "attempt to categorize the parables as tragic and comic seems somewhat artificial," and not clearly appropriate to the parables,[44] since it requires the use of terminology out of place in Jesus' Palestinian world. This criticism does not necessarily nullify Via's analysis of the parable types, however, since, in principle, there is no reason such categories cannot be applied to the parables. Nevertheless, as noted above, the parables may not respond easily to such literary "typing." Via's own irresolution as to whether the Laborers in the Vineyard was a comic or tragic parable is a case in point. For Via, it turned out to be a comic parable. Were Herzog to "type" it using Via's categories, however, he would no doubt call it a tragic parable,[45] and even Via himself had to admit that "in a sense it should have been discussed with the tragic parables."[46] This suggests that literary "typing" of these parables is as likely due to a particular reader's response to the narrative as to some quantitative element in the story. Literary criticism is more an art than a science.

Via's argument that the parables are aesthetic objects has been challenged as invalid, because every parable of Jesus clearly "was designed to have reference to a specific situation in his ministry."[47] It is likely true that Jesus designed the parables for specific historical situations; he was not creating art for art's sake. But scholars have no sure knowledge what those specific situations were, and know the historical circumstances of Jesus' life only in the most general way. What is needed are more sources, as well as a refinement of methods. Thus, Via's idea that the parables are "aesthetic objects" comes close to describing the actual situation faced by modern readers of the parables. We have the artistic creations but know next to nothing about why he created them, or the specific situations for which they were created. To offset the fact that we simply do not know the specific contexts in which the parables were spoken, scholars usually assume some kind of context in his life as a specific backdrop for reading the parables, as Jeremias and Herzog did, for example.[48] Virtually every interpreter of the parables assumes something as background for the reading of particular parables.

Via's theory that the parables contain particular understandings of human existence fails to accommodate all the parables, since it does not allow for the nature parables, which do not treat human activity.[49] In the nature parables discussion of human existence must be imported into the parable. This criticism, however, does not invalidate his recognition of the existential dimension to other parables. In any case, Via never claims that his treatment of the parables is what Jesus *intended.* He only claims that "the many elements of the parable *within* their pattern of connections as a *whole* imply an understanding of existence."[50] It is the nature of literature, in other words. Authors of artistic works, by the very nature of literature, say more than they intend;[51] hence, the parables may legitimately be analyzed from this perspective irrespective of Jesus' intention. But a theory that will not accommodate all the parables has serious limitations.

Via has justifiably been highly lauded for his literary criticism of the parables: "With the appearance of Via's book in 1967 the interpretation of the parables took on a new dimension. It [is] obviously the most important book on parables since Jeremias," one scholar said.[52] He went on to say that whereas we learned from Jeremias about the historical approach to the parables, Via teaches us the limitations of that approach, and opens a new door to the parables through literary criticism.

PARABLES AS POETIC FICTIONS: CHARLES W. HEDRICK

My own book argues that parables are brief, realistic, narrative fictions, freely invented from observations of typical first-century Palestinian peasant life. They work like all realistic narrative does: Their plots are intended to engage readers for themselves and to draw readers out of their own world into the parable's fictional world.[53] Parables *may* have referential quality, but this must be argued for each parable; the attribution of referential quality may not simply be assumed. Their deliberate referentiality hinges on the successful identification of specific triggers *within* the narrative, which can be shown to propel the mind out of the narrative in an identifiable *particular* direction, and on the verification of those triggers as deliberate sanctions for the figurative leaps to other planes of reality. Otherwise readers are mandated to remain within the parable's narrative world, discussing the parable by using the language of the parable itself. The further an interpreter digresses from the language of the parable, explaining it using language other than that provided by the parable, the less convincing the interpretation is as a historical explanation. Reducing parables to an abstraction is a reader's response to the parable; abstractions cannot provide readers the same experience as the parable.

The comparative frames and interpretations that introduce and conclude some of the parables do not come from Jesus, but represent early Christian attempts to tweak an appropriate Christian interpretation from these essentially secular Jewish stories.[54]

The parables are stories about common life in the first century, but they are scarcely banal. In the first century, they "subverted, affirmed, and confronted the broader views of reality on the basis of which first-century human beings conducted their lives."[55] Jesus' parables are the products of common first-century realities and an uncommon imagination, and they still have "the potential of igniting the imaginations of those who consent to enter [Jesus'] fictional world."[56]

As narrative, the parables are like chameleons; they become what readers want them to become—as the history of parables research frighteningly demonstrates.[57] They can be allegories, metaphors, or example stories, according to the learned whims of the interpreters; they can teach a moral lesson or reveal dimensions of human existence. What they become depends on what the interpreter decides to make of them. Their polyvalence gives them their chameleon-like character. Many things happen even in short fictions; this diversity prompts different readers to see different things in them. Thus, there will never be one final authoritative reading of a parable that can exclude all others, for the polyvalence of the parable continually undermines interpretations by suggesting new possibilities to new readers—particularly as culture, society, and circumstances change. The best that can be hoped is that scholars will achieve a consensus on a range of plausible historical readings. (A plausible historical reading is the way a first-century Palestinian Jew might have responded to the parable.) The poetics of the parable (how it is constructed) played off against a general social reconstruction of the Palestine of Jesus' time may limit the range of plausible readings to some extent.

The parables of Jesus are open-ended; they have no conclusions that tell readers how to react. Indeed, they seem designed to present readers with deliberate conundrums; how to resolve these conundrums is what has driven the history of parables research. Parables make no value judgments on characters or their activities. The narrative voice of the parables has neither conscience nor morals; it shows the drama, letting characters and action pass without judgmental comment. Readers make sense of a parable, or not, out of what they bring to it—just as Jesus' first auditors were forced to do. The meaning of the parable is not *inside* the parable, but meaning is developed by readers who interact with the parable. The parable is not closed until the auditor/reader is drawn into it as participant,[58] or, as Funk puts it, "The 'meaning' of the parable [of the Samaritan] is the way auditors take up roles in the story and play out the drama."[59] To give a parable an authoritative interpretation—to tell the reader how to "take it"—subverts the parable by closing off a reader's participation and preventing the parable from witnessing in its own way to each reader.[60]

The parables have the potential to work today just as they did for auditors in the first century, who made sense of them, or not, in terms of who they were and what they brought to the audition. The stories either resonated with first-century auditors or not.[61] "Resonance" describes the interaction of auditor and parable. It is a concept in phonetics (the science or study of speech sounds) and describes the prolongation of sound by reverberation and reflection—an amplification of the range of the audibility of sounds. Put another way, sound reverberates—and so do ideas and parables. When effective, artistic narrative works in a similar way. Parables resonate with readers whose engagement with the story provokes reflection. In this way, the parable raises for the reader awareness of issues not technically a part of the narrative. Put another way, the parable *evokes* issues for particular readers. Using still another image, the parable lifts the reader's horizon of understanding; it raises the reader's "range of vision" beyond the narrow limits of the story. The reader glimpses things *suggested to that particular reader* by the parable in the nexus between parable and reader—that is to say, in the reader's reflection on the parable. In that nexus (i.e., in the reader's mind reflecting on the story within the parable's world) readers find affirmation, challenge, or subversion to the constructs under which they conduct their own lives. If effective, the parable suggests to them a broader vision of life's possibilities, a different way of being in the world. Frank Kermode said, "Fictions are for finding things out,"[62] and that has certainly been true of the parables of Jesus, to judge from the incredible breadth of things interpreters have discovered.

The Parable of a Fig Tree in a Vineyard (Luke 13:6–9) as Read by Hedrick

This parable presents itself as a problem in farm management—what to do with a fig tree barren for three years.[63] Luke does not provide an interpretation, but the parable's position following Luke 13:1–5 suggests that Luke understood it as a parable of judgment (cf. Luke 13:3, 5, 9). The sheer secularity of the story, however, is a strong contrast to Luke 13:1–5. What Jesus thought of this story, and, indeed, of all his parables, has been lost since the first century—if it was ever known.

The narrative has four phases—*situation*: a man had a fig tree in his vineyard (13:6a); *complication*: it had not borne figs for three years (13:6b–7a); *resolution*: the owner orders it cut down (13:7b); *a new complication*: the vintner proposes another, less radical, solution (13:8–9). In order to be complete, the narrative now needs a resolution. The owner must make a new decision: Does he follow the vintner's suggestion or not?

Readers are provided no direct information about the owner. A close reader may be struck by the oddity of a single fig tree in a vineyard. Actually fig trees in vineyards were common occurrences in antiquity; they were used for trellising grapevines, as well as for bearing figs. Thus, this fig tree has a reason for existing other than simply bearing figs. There could be many reasons why the tree had not borne figs: Maybe it is too young or has been overwatered; perhaps it has not been fertilized or received proper care. Sterility of trees is a common problem, but, in general, untended trees do not bear fruit.[64] Three years of unfruitfulness simply underlines the fact that unless something is done this tree is unlikely to bear in the immediate future.

The owner's decision to cut it down (13:7) seems radical, especially if the tree were being used as a trellis for vines—which would surely have been the case for competent farmers. In any case, the tree was not completely useless, as even the vintner's response to the owner (13:8) suggests. The owner's rationale for cutting down the tree seems rather laughable; trees cut down will sprout back as long as they are not uprooted. The vintner clearly disagrees with the owner's decision to cut down the tree, and asks for a chance to tend the tree for another year. But he is a vintner who knows vines; the reader can only wonder who really knows more about trees, vintner or owner? Ancient farming manuals suggest a variety of treatments for ailing trees, and what the vintner suggests (digging and manuring) is essential annual care for trees.[65] The ellipsis in 13:9 ("and if it bears fruit in the future . . .") serves to heighten the uncertainty both of the owner's decision and the tree's future. How does a reader take the vintner's response (13:9, "*you* will cut it down")—as sarcasm, incredulity, acquiescence, or insubordination? The expected response of a servant is "Yes sir, *I* will cut it down, as you direct."

The story focuses on phase four, the new complication. The owner's decision to cut down the tree appears uninformed for the reasons stated above. The vintner thinks the problem can be fixed, however. The problem for the reader is: Who knows more? The vintner knows enough to suggest minimal treatment, but if he had tried those things in previous years he would know they would not work again this year. Hence, even the vintner seems a somewhat flawed character. The fig tree seems to be at the mercy of an owner and vintner who have neglected its care, neither of whom seem to know nearly enough about fig trees. To some extent the owner can be excused, but the vintner clearly knew better, to judge from his suggestion about tending the tree. At the very least, we may conclude the owner seems to be incompetent and the vintner not highly motivated in his job.[66]

There is no way to know for certain how first-century auditors might have responded to the story. People who viewed life religiously in terms of Torah may have heard it in terms of blessing and judgment. Flourishing vines and fruitful fig trees symbolize God's blessing; thus, the owner's neighbors might have regarded him as "a sinner" under God's judgment on the basis of his barren fig tree. On the other hand, another pious auditor might have taken the story to be a warning about exhausting God's patience and his near judgment. Farmers in the audience, however, might simply have heard it as a humorous story about two incompetent farmers.[67] Not even Jesus could control how people understood him.

I read the narrative as a story of hope. The story is not about the tree but about two flawed farmers who did nothing to help the tree. The owner's response to the vintner's suggestion (Luke 13:8) will actually determine the nature of the story, but the narrator stops the story before the owner decides, providing no solution to the conundrum. If the tree is cut down, the story is about judgment. If it is allowed to live, the story is about renewed life and the potential productivity of the tree. Because there is no resolution, the story remains open. In the ellipsis (13:9), however, flickers a tiny ray of hope—the story's eternal legacy, which is always there every time the story is read. Hope does seem to characterize the three stories that follow the parable: the healing of the bent woman, the tiny mustard seed that became a tree, and the pinch of yeast that caused a bushel of flour to rise.[68] An enterprising reader might abstract the story as follows: In the blackest moment there is always a faint ray of hope—but such an abstraction scarcely replaces the experience of the story itself. Because the story is open-ended and polyvalent, it will clearly resonate differently with other readers.

Critique

Reviews of my book were generally favorable, although there were criticisms, such as: The value of the poetics section was unclear;[69] Hedrick is too optimistic that Jesus was a creative person; he gives the impression that first-century Judaism was a monolithic structure; accurate knowledge of the period is too scanty to allow use of it to represent the fictional constructs of first-century Jews; his interpretations boil down to finding "meanings" again; his readings are suggestive but a little forced; his "entire method is assumed rather than demonstrated."[70]

Amos Wilder, on the other hand, offered a corrective to the idea that the comparative frames of the parables derive from the early church. "In the light of his thorough documentation of the way in which the tradition construed these parables Hedrick can plausibly conclude that the church had soon forgotten or misconstrued their original situation and import."[71] While the parables may not directly refer outside of themselves (as I have argued), Wilder reasoned that I would grant that the parable "awoke some kind of *resonance* in the hearers."[72] Wilder qualifies my "conjecture that the early church had lost touch with . . . the original meaning of Jesus' parables" by urging "that their original force . . . continued in a kind of underground way in the memory of the community."[73]

In the following way, Wilder seeks to reestablish the linkage between the early church and its founder. Jesus' "fictions have specific traits in their composition and vision which evoke a particular perspective."[74] This perspective may be preconceptual, but at that early level it is implicitly normative—meaning that Jesus' perspective is an innate part of the parables. The later tradition drew on the parables and the "normative perspective" reflected in the parables, and made connection with Jesus through the response evoked by the parables. So the parables were not "open to a gratuitous free play of signification." Wilder puts it this way: "If, indeed, as seems likely, the later tradition rightly traced in some of [the parables] a correlation with the Kingdom of God, we can agree with Hedrick that it would have been in terms of imaginative evocation rather than metaphorical comparison."[75] Wilder is reluctant to admit a complete loss of the "original force and horizon" of the parables with respect to the canonical tradition, but allows for that possibility, when the "eschatological perspective of Jesus' mission" has been missed—specifically in the case of wisdom traditions and gnostic speculation.[76] The continuation of the "normative perspective" of the parables by the later Christian tradition, which Wilder insists on, raises the question: What exactly is the "normative perspective" of the parables? With that question, we have gone full circle to where this book began.

10

How Does a Parable Resonate?

Empowering the Reader

At the end of the day, a parable speaks in its own way to an attentive reader. As Amos Wilder said:

> A work of art has a life of its own apart from its reporters. It remains itself and goes on testifying or celebrating, independently of its interpreters and their various versions and deformations of its communication. So it is with a parable or other literary form in Scripture. Its *telling* is ever and again to be heard naively and afresh. The deep registers of response in the hearer should not be disturbed at this level of encounter by other preoccupations.[1]

In other words, the parable's voice is what it says to individual readers in its unqualified state. Permitting a parable to resonate—to find its own voice—is not as easy as it may sound, however. Wilder suggests that readers focus on the parable and not allow hearing to be distracted "by other preoccupations"—for example, the interpretations of critics, who tend to impose their own responses to the parable on their readers as the authoritative reading.

Because parables are sayings of Jesus, readers expect a great deal from them—and the parables seldom fail to disappoint the expectations of readers. Yet the many differences among what readers expect and find raise the question: Whose voice is being heard—the interpreter's voice or the parable's? This chapter proposes a guide for listening to parables; it is designed to facilitate an engagement between parable and reader to allow the parable to resonate in its own way. Readers do not have to be Bible experts, know the biblical languages of Greek and Hebrew, or be experts in ancient culture in order to appreciate the distinctive "voice" of a parable. Few, if any, of Jesus' first auditors were experts; his parables were addressed to a peasant population for the most part. The first auditors did not need the learned critic to explain a parable; as Wilder said, a parable speaks in its own way to each auditor, and in our day, to each reader. Of course it helps to have all the linguistic and scholarly skills, but they are not essential to appreciating the parables. This listener's guide leads the reader through a series of steps that aim to put the reader in the audience at a parable's first audition. All that is required of the reader is a little work and a willingness to set aside about two thousand years of Christian history, so as to hear the parable with a fresh naïveté. Many readers will likely be unable to divest themselves of their Christian history, but it is an absolutely essential first step to joining the crowd at Jesus' feet. Not a single Christian shared in the first audition of his stories.

STEP ONE: SEPARATE THE PARABLE FROM ITS LITERARY CONTEXT

A parable will never speak in its own way as long as it is embedded in a literary context. Thus, identifying the precise limits of the story is the first step. In general, this step is usually easy to accomplish. The reader must remember that the parable is a story within a story—a story told by Jesus, who, as we encounter him in the gospels, is a character in another story. For example, the parable of the Samaritan (Luke 10:30b–35) is a story told by Luke's character, Jesus, whom Luke portrays debating with a Torah expert. In this case, the difference between the two "worlds" is crystal clear. The reader leaves Luke's story about Jesus (i.e., Luke's Gospel) and enters the parable's story about a robbery on the road to Jericho (i.e., the parable of the Samaritan) immediately after the words "Jesus replied" (Luke 10:30). The reader again reenters Luke's story about Jesus at the conclusion of Luke 10:35; the shift is clearly marked, since Luke 10:36 is a question directed to the expert on the law in Luke's story. Luke 10:36 is not addressed to any of the characters in Jesus' story about the Samaritan. Thus, the story of the Samaritan consists of Luke 10:30b–35.

Reflections on the story, statements about the story, and evaluations of the story—of its characters and action—by definition are never part of the parable. Since evaluations look back at the parable from a different perspective, they are always *outside* the parable. For example, Luke 18:14—"I tell you [i.e., some who trusted in themselves, alluded to in 18:9] this man [probably the toll collector in Jesus' story] went down to his house justified rather than the other"—is an evaluation by Luke's Jesus of the actors *inside* the story of the Pharisee and toll collector (18:10–13) from a vantage point *outside* the story. By definition, such outside evaluations cannot be part of the parable; rather, they are part of Luke's story about Jesus.

Literary introductions and conclusions to the parable are likewise not a part of the story. For example, Luke sets the story about the Lost Sheep (15:4–7) in the literary context of an accusation scribes and Pharisees made against Jesus. "This fellow welcomes sinners and eats with them," they say (15:2). Then Luke's Jesus tells the story (15:4–7) in response to the criticism (15:3). After the story is finished, Luke's Jesus draws the conclusion "Just so, I tell you, there will be more joy in heaven over one sinner who repents than over ninety-nine righteous persons who need no repentance" (15:7).[2] The conclusion is not part of the story but a reflection on the story.

Comparative introductory frames that instruct readers to draw comparisons are likewise not inside the parable's world; rather, they are instructions within the evangelist's story, telling readers contemporary with Luke how the evangelist expects the story to be heard. For example, Matt 13:44a ("For the kingdom of heaven is like . . ."), introducing the parable of a Treasure in a Field, is Matthew's guidance to the reader of his gospel; it is not a part of the story about a treasure hidden in a field.

STEP TWO: WHAT IS THE TEXTUAL HISTORY OF THE PARABLE?

Now that the limits of the story are clearly defined, the reader knows precisely where to focus. This second step requires a bit of work. If there is only one version of the parable, like the parable of the Steward (Luke 16:1–7), this step is somewhat easier to accomplish. Multiple versions of the story, like the Sower (Matt 13:3b–9; Mark 4:3b–8; Luke 8:5–8a), however, require more work. At this point the reader needs to know if there are variations between the different versions. The goal is to determine what version of the story should be considered. Subtle differences between the versions cause the reader/auditor to hear and see different things.

One-Version Parables

One-version parables require examining the transmission history of the single story. Do versions of the story in ancient manuscripts have significant variations? If so, these variations suggest the different ways the story was understood in antiquity. Unfortunately, however, modern translators do not always make this information available to readers in the form of notes to the translation. Such a note signals the modern reader that sufficient doubt exists about which ancient reading is preferred; the preferred reading appears in the text and the note provides an alternative reading, which could well be original.

Variations in the texts of ancient manuscripts reveal different ways the parable was understood in the early centuries of the Christian era.

Sometimes, however, different scribal readings in the ancient manuscripts are revealed to the modern language reader. This happens only when different modern translations follow the readings of different manuscripts. For example, most modern translations of the parable of the Two Sons (Matt 21:28b–30) have the parable as follows:

> A man had two sons; and he went to the first and said, "Son, go and work in the vineyard today." And he answered, "I will not"; but afterward he repented and went. And he went to the second and said the same; and he answered, "I go, sir," but did not go. (RSV)

The New American Bible (1970), however, has the following translation:

> There was a man who had two sons. He approached the elder and said, "Son, go out and work in the vineyard today." The son replied, "I am on my way, sir"; but he never went. Then the man came to his second son and said the same thing. This son said in reply, "No, I will not"; but afterward he regretted it and went.

The manuscripts also vary on the answer that the interlocutors give to Jesus' question in Matt 21:31. Most translations read "The first" (the "appropriate" response to the RSV version); the New American Bible, however, reads "the second" (the "appropriate" response to its version of the parable). These responses, which are not a part of the parable, imply a particular understanding of it. For example, the "appropriate response" values actions over words. A brief discussion of these significant textual variations in the ancient manuscripts can be found in Bruce Metzger's *A Textual Commentary on the Greek New Testament*.[3]

Multiple-Version Parables

In many cases, multiple versions of the same parable exist in the literature. The parable of the Lost Sheep, for example, exists in three versions: Matt 18:12b–13; Luke 15:4–6; *Thom.* 107. Each of these versions is actually a different performance of the same story. In order to understand the different ways this parable was understood in Christian antiquity, readers must make a careful comparison between them, looking for even the smallest difference. These differences aid modern readers in understanding how ancient readers "heard" the parable.[4] Of course a comparison of different performances raises the question of originality: Which is the earliest version of the parable? Aids exist for addressing this issue,[5] but each version is important for its witness to one early Christian understanding of the parable. At some point, however, each reader will have to decide which version to investigate more closely.

STEP THREE: CONSIDER THE ELEMENTS OF THE STORY—LINE BY LINE, WORD BY WORD

Having decided which parable is to be analyzed, the reader consults as many different modern translations of the parable in as many different languages as competence allows. This is important because a translation is also a translator's interpretation. Readers must deal with two levels to every parable—what the ancient text said in the original language and what the modern translator construes it to be saying. There is no such thing as a literal translation from one language to another, but some translations can be more interpretive than others. For this reason more than one translation of the parable must be read.

At this step, the reader asks questions about aspects of the story as a part of the ancient Palestinian world—meaning that the reader aims to "hear" the elements of the parable as a part of Jesus' world and not as a part of the modern reader's world. Nothing may be taken for granted; everything in the parable must be treated as though it were foreign to the reader's world. For example, what exactly are the "pods" that the younger son eats in the foreign country (Luke 15:16)? Is it customary for a father to provide his children their inheritance before the father dies (Luke 15:12)? What is a mustard seed (Mark 4:31)? Are they really the "smallest of all the seeds on earth"? If they are not, does that make a difference? Do mustard plants grow up to become trees (Luke 13:19)? What is a single fig tree doing in a vineyard (Luke 13:6)? What exactly is a steward and how much power were such persons delegated (Luke 16:1)? What kind of seeds did the farmer sow, and what result should the farmer expect from his field (Matt 13:8)? Is the harvest of this farmer's field (Mark 4:8) a lot, a little, or simply usual? Is it normal for a shepherd to leave his flock untended in the wilderness (Luke 15:3)? In other words, how do the elements of the parable resonate in the socioeconomic world of first-century Palestine—how would a Palestinian audience have understood them?

A competent Bible dictionary can provide answers to many of these questions. For example, if the question concerns plants, the reader will find a helpful entry on "flora" in the *Anchor Bible Dictionary*, with additional bibliography.[6] In addition, the reader will most certainly need to consult the commentaries on the gospels, in which individual parables are discussed.[7] But at this point the reader must ignore how interpreters evaluate the significance of these elements. Reading the commentaries at this stage is only for the purpose of gathering raw data about the ancient world and trying to determine how the various elements of the parable fit into that world.

STEP FOUR: EXAMINE THE LITERARY FEATURES OF THE NARRATIVE

Next, the reader evaluates the parable as a narrative. The reader must describe the plot and the characters—that is, describe *in the language of the story* what is going on *inside* the story—but, at this stage, he or she must do so without passing moral judgment on the characters or their actions. In short, this step requires a neutral retelling of the story. Were any gaps of any sort discovered in the narrative? What is the time frame in which the story occurs? Does anything in the story seem to reflect a lack of realism? Does the narrative use anything that might be considered figurative language? What is surprising in this narrative? Does anything strike you as odd? What are you curious about in this story? Is the story brought to a conclusion, or is the reader left hanging, wondering what happened next?

STEP FIVE: HYPOTHETICAL RESPONSE(S) OF A FIRST-CENTURY JEWISH AUDIENCE

This is probably the most difficult step to accomplish. The reader needs to be familiar with sources that describe first-century Palestinian Judaism. Written sources for Judaism in the first century are limited. Essentially they are the Hebrew Bible, the Jewish Apocrypha, the Pseudepigrapha, the Dead Sea Scrolls, and the writings of Philo and Josephus. There are also other valuable Jewish sources that were not written down until about two hundred years or more after the period of Christian origins.[8]

Lack of familiarity with these materials will seriously hamper a historical reading of the parable. To some extent, however, a general familiarity with the period can be gained by reading the Jewish backgrounds section in a competent introduction to the New Testament.[9] Competent Bible dictionaries can also provide more detailed information about specific texts in the collections of literature cited above and specific aspects of first-century Judaism. The major thing to remember is that Christian readings of the parables are anachronisms; first-century Palestinian Jews would have heard the parables with first-century Palestinian Jewish ears.

STEP SIX: HOW DOES THE READER RESPOND TO THE PARABLE?

The modern reader's own personal reaction to the story is just one response among many. A reader's response should never be construed as the ultimate meaning of the parable, for there have been many responses to the parable, and there will be others in the future. The parable's "voice" is how it resonates in its own way for each reader. As there were different responses to Jesus' stories in the first century, so there are different responses to them today—as the history of parables interpretation unequivocally demonstrates. A reader's response occurs in the nexus between the parable and the life experience the reader brings to it; hopefully it will also include informed reflection on the parable.

In thinking about the parable and discussing it, readers should be careful to use the language of the parable itself. I have said this repeatedly throughout the book. Using the parable's language keeps the reader inside the story. Evaluating the actions of a character in the story should stay with the language and information provided by the story. The reader's abstraction of the parable is a reader's response; it is what the parable has evoked for that particular reader.

ILLUSTRATING THE STEPS: THE PARABLE OF THE RICH FARMER (LUKE 12:16b–1920/21; *THOM* 63)

Step 1: Where the story begins is clear in Luke's version: Luke 12:16b.[10] The ending is not as clear, however. Luke 12:21 is clearly outside the story because it provides a judgment on the entire story; it is the conclusion of Luke's character, Jesus. But the voice in Luke 12:20 is different. This voice passes judgment on the rich farmer in the story,[11] and is one of only two instances in the entire parables corpus where a character is described by a negative appellation and attribute.[12] Thus, it is suspect as Luke's intrusion into the parable, and that being the case, provides the reader with Luke's response. Further, it is not really a part of the dramatic action of the story about the farmer for two reasons: The farmer apparently never hears the voice of God; only the reader does. The divine pronouncement (12:20) has the character of an outside judgment on the story (God is not an actor in this story), which is characteristic of the *epimythia* (summary conclusions) in the gospels. Thus, where the story concludes is not so easily resolved. Does it conclude at 12:19 or 12:20? The reader must decide the issue, and how it is resolved will significantly impact how the story is read.

Step 2: This is a two-version parable; perhaps even a third version exists. A close parallel to Luke's story is found in Sirach 11:18–19. The stories in Sirach and Luke/*Thomas* are similar, but also different in a number of ways. In an earlier study, I concluded that they were not the same story and that the story in Sirach influenced Luke's telling of the story. As I look at it today, it seems likely that Sirach may actually have prompted Luke's addition of God's voice

(12:20) pronouncing judgment on the rich farmer in the story. In any case, I decided in my earlier analysis that the stories in Luke and *Thomas* were two different performances from the same originating structure and that Luke's version was closest to the original structure.[13] Today, I am not as sure. It seems likely that *Thomas*'s version may represent the earliest and that Luke, under the influence of Sirach 11:18–19, revised it. Luke replaced the earlier version's statement (appearing in *Thomas*) "so that I lack nothing" with Sirach's 11:19a, "I have found rest, and now I shall feast on my goods" (cf. Luke 12:19a). Luke further added "eat, drink, be merry" (12:19b); these words are well known in Jewish literature, where they are used not negatively but positively to characterize the culmination of a blessed life.[14] Luke then added 12:20, which forces the reader to hear Luke 12:19 in a negative light.

Steps 3 and 4: A line-by-line, word-by-word analysis of Luke 12:16b–20 should bring to light new information about the parable's social world. "The 'estate' of a rich man produced abundantly." This man is clearly a member of the elite class—he is no peasant farmer. He has an unexpected and unusual harvest, which (as readers learn in the next line) his storage facilities could not accommodate. "And he thought to himself, 'What should I do, for I have no place to store my crops?' " This is an important line. It tells the reader that the farmer has crops in the field ready for harvesting; the recognition of the need for additional storage space occurs at the precise moment he should be gathering in the crops. So why didn't the farmer recognize some weeks earlier there was going to be an unusual harvest and begin preparations at that time to accommodate the crop? The reader must fill in this gap in some way: Is it an oversight on Luke's part? Has Luke been careless in writing the story? Is it a deliberate attempt by Luke to describe the farmer ironically (i.e., this farmer is so incompetent he didn't read his fields correctly until the actual moment of harvest)? Also, the farmer is only concerned about his wheat; there is no mention of the other crops, such as grain, grapes, and olives. Is this just one more oversight by the farmer? Is the narrator trying to focus the story on the wheat harvest? If so, what are the "goods" (12:19) the farmer hopes to store in the new buildings?

"I will pull down my storage facilities and build larger ones."[15] The storage facilities he intends to tear down and rebuild are granaries, in which he intends to store other things as well (i.e., "goods"). Here again is another curiosity. Why does the farmer decide to tear down perfectly good storage facilities and build larger ones, at the very time he should be gathering in his harvest? Such a plan makes the farmer look a little foolish. Has the narrator done that by design or carelessness?

"And I will say to myself, 'Self, you have many good things laid up for many years' " (author's translation). He plans to store his crops, as every farmer does.

That is the reason, after all, why farmers have storage facilities. Storing crops for future use or future markets, when prices are better, is the way farmers benefit from unusual harvests. "Take it easy, eat, drink, enjoy yourself" (author's translation). In themselves, these words are neutral, as anyone who saves money for retirement clearly realizes. The only wise course of action is to plan for the future, and most people do that. This farmer is no exception.

"That night he died," and never had the opportunity of doing what he intended. Here I take over the ending to *Thomas*'s story, assuming that Luke has dropped an original ending and replaced it with Luke 12:20. It is possible, however, that the story actually ended with Luke 12:19, leaving a reader wondering what happened next, as is the case with Luke 13:6b–9. I cannot seriously consider Luke 12:20 as an original ending to the parable, however, for the reasons given above. Anyone retaining Luke 12:20 as the original ending should set out an affirmative argument why that is so, since it does not play any part in the dramatic action of the story of the rich farmer.

Step 5: Of course, the story can be heard in different ways. The goal in this section is to present a plausible way that a first-century Jew might have heard the story, based on available information about the period.[16] In the Hebrew Bible wealth is viewed both affirmative and negatively. On the one hand, wealth and prosperity were seen as the blessings of God. On the other, however, the rich are seen as wicked, perverse, and haughty. True "riches" for the pious Israelite was wisdom. Because of the great distance between the wealthy and the poor (i.e., no middle class existed in ancient Judaism), this story may well have resonated with Jesus' audience as an anti-upper-class story. The man's bumbling and inappropriate actions would have delighted an audience who thought critically of the wealthy. The man's death on the very evening he thought things were going so well would reaffirm for pious Jews in the audience the inability of material wealth to protect even the wealthy and, by contrast, affirm the pursuit of true riches—wisdom and Torah.

On the other hand, the story seems most at home in the cynical tradition of Ecclesiastes, where Qoheleth comforts himself with the simple pleasures of life. While Qoheleth certainly perseveres in his faith, he "hardly champions the meaningfulness of life."[17] Jesus' dark story raises the question of life's meaning, just as Qoheleth did. And Luke may be one ancient reader who actually heard it that way. Luke recasts the farmer in the story as a man for whom life consisted in laying up treasure for himself rather than being "rich" toward God (Luke 12:21). According to Luke, the wealthy farmer in the story had his priorities wrong.

Step 6: Now readers are in a position to make their own thoughtful response. How does the story resonate—that is, how does it affect the reader and how does the reader respond to the story? For my part, I still find the story quite humorous; it is burlesque—a caricature of a wealthy bumbling farmer raising a serious question.

The entire story takes place at harvesttime in the brief moment the farmer suddenly realizes that he has misjudged the extent of his crop. He has a bumper crop needing to be gathered in immediately, but he has insufficient storage space. Weighing his various options, he comes up with a laughably inappropriate action, given the fact that the crop is standing in the field and ready for harvest.[18] He plans to tear down what storage facilities he has and begin building new facilities—with his crops in the field ready for harvest! Tearing down existing facilities is the one thing he definitely should not do, since it is time to harvest his crop.

He also makes another more serious miscalculation. He misjudges the length of his life, assuming he will live several more years—at least until he has enjoyed some of the benefits of this unexpected bounty. Alas, it soon becomes clear that his brief fantasy (12:19) is all he will enjoy of the harvest. That evening he dies, with "his fields overflowing with abundance and his storage facilities yet unmodified."[19]

For me, the story raises the issues of life's meaning and priorities in a dramatic way, but it offers no answers. What is completely clear from the story, however, is that economic prosperity does not provide a sense of deep satisfaction with life. Here is a man who, on the very day of his death, was preoccupied with things, which in eternity's long sweep have virtually no significance at all. Economic prosperity may satisfy the need for creature comforts, but what does it do for the complete human being? Or as Mark's Jesus says, "What does it profit a human being to gain the whole world and forfeit the essential self?" (Mark 8:36; author's translation). "Self" implies that human beings are more than creatures—more than simple sinew, flesh, and bone. They have needs other than creature comforts—emotional, mental, spiritual, and psychological needs. Human beings also need a sense of purpose and acceptance. They need to feel that life has purpose; they need to share life with others. Surely there is more in life for "self" than sowing, planting, harvesting, and dying. This story about the death of a wealthy farmer evokes such issues for me.

Readers usually demand more of the narrative voice of the parables than the raising of questions. They want answers as well—in what should my life be invested, if not economic prosperity? But the narrator does not answer, at least not directly. The terrifying image of a man who "had it made"—only to lose it all on the very eve of his success—leaves the reader groping for something more, looking for some deeper purpose, for some overarching rationale to everything, some comfort, something, anything to mitigate the tragedy of the story. This parable's very secularity raises these issues for everyone—the religious person, as well as the materialist. No one is immune to the probing question raised by the story: In what does life consist, if not economic prosperity? The parable's witness is a call to engage the question.

Epilogue

In 1994 I found myself on a trajectory taking me out of what I described as "the mainstream" of parables interpretation. As I look back over the past ten years and what I say in this current book, the term "mainstream" is neither precise nor accurate. At the time, I was thinking about critical studies of parables. But the field is much broader than that. Use of parables in many, if not most, ecclesiastical contexts today tend not to be informed by critical studies, and would have to be described as pre-Jülicher in method. Parables study among many scholars who have closely identified themselves with ecclesiastical contexts, institutions, or concerns tend to be more conservative and traditional—even evangelistic. In short, parables study today is all over the board, and scholars who have published studies of the parables in the last thirty years or so seem to be in agreement about very few things. And it does not appear that anything like a consensus will be achieved in the near future—if ever.

The failure of contemporary studies to achieve consensus, or even near consensus, is surprising, because until Jülicher's book (1888), a virtual unanimous consensus existed on what parables were and how they functioned: They were allegories teaching Christian truths. Jülicher's book discredited allegory—in my judgment even limited allegory—as a responsible way to read parables, and that left a vacuum—at least it did for critical scholars. For over one hundred years now, critical scholars have been experimenting with various new approaches without much agreement on a preferable method. Perhaps it is time to begin narrowing the field by seeking the common ground between them. Toward that end, I briefly set out here the observations and the rationale leading me out of the mainstream of critical studies—and far outside traditional approaches. These observations still seem cogent to me today, and therefore a good place to begin dialogue.

WE DO NOT KNOW HOW JESUS USED HIS PARABLES

This basic observation seems rather obvious to me for the following reasons: All we have from Jesus, if anything, are the parables. We generally accept that the earliest versions of the parables were first written down in the second half of the first century by second-generation Christians in a cultural context and language different from that in which they were first spoken. Without question, the earliest exemplars of parables are found in third-century manuscripts and later. Thus, so far as we know and can reasonably show, explanations of parables in the gospels derive from second-generation Christians who first wrote them down decades after the time of Jesus. The evangelists agree neither on what the parables said, nor on their meaning.

THE COMPARATIVE FRAMES ARE NOT IN THE PARABLE

The comparative frames to the parables are actually part of the evangelists' story about Jesus; they are not part of Jesus' stories about village life. Thus, they are part of the evangelists' literary contexts and strategies, which include *promythia* and *epimythia*. As such, they belong to a later period of the early Christian movement—Hellenistic Christianity—rather than to the fictional world of Jesus' parables. The comparative frames tell us how second-generation Christians used the parables rather than how Jesus used them. Half the stories attributed to Jesus in early Christian literature do not have comparative frames. The association of the story with the "reign of God" comes only in the comparative frames, and because they fall outside the parable, the frames should, at the very least, be suspect as a later Christian attempt to make religious sense of very secular stories. In short, the "reign of God" should not be made the essential hermeneutical key to the parables. Only thirteen stories in all versions associate the parable with the reign of God; twenty-five stories are not associated with the reign of God in a comparative frame.

THE FIGURATIVE CHARACTER OF PARABLES MAY NOT SIMPLY BE ASSUMED

This observation is driven by the fact that the stories of Jesus are not inherently figurative. As the history of parables interpretation unambiguously shows, parables work any way interpreters and auditors want them to work—in spite of whatever Jesus may have intended with them in their oral early phase. Since we simply do not know how Jesus used parables and clearly have no hope of ever discovering his intention, the issue of how they are used should not be solved by an assumption. It is the nature of narrative to be used any way the storyteller wishes to use it. It is the nature of narrative to lend itself to an auditor's imagination and become whatever the auditor wants it to be—in spite of the narrator's intention. Narratives are essentially polyvalent, and therefore subject to a wide range of readings.

EVERY INTERPRETATION OF A PARABLE IS A PARTICULAR READER'S RESPONSE

In the light of my first observation, how could I think otherwise? Interpreters of parables are not telling readers what Jesus actually meant with the parable; they simply do not, and cannot, know that. Interpreters describe what *they think* Jesus meant—something vastly different. An explanation is evoked in a particular reader's mind from an engagement with a parable, and responses depend as much on what that interpreter brings to the parable as on what the parable itself says—perhaps more so. Had the interpreter been present in the audience when Jesus first spoke the parable, the situation would have been no different. My hypothetical modern interpreter, whom I have just taken back in time to the feet of Jesus, would still have to make sense of the parable as interpreters do today. Then as now, others in the audience would have had rather different responses. In this sense the situation with interpretations of parables today is identical to what would have been the case in the first century. Thus, no "right" interpretations of the parables of Jesus ever existed. By "right" I mean interpretations that capture Jesus' intent. Given the nature of narrative, no one explanation of a parable can rule out all others. This conclusion is confirmed by the construction of the parables themselves: With no conclusions or value judgments built into them, they are always subject to a variety of readings.

These observations raise the specter of anarchy in the interpretation of the parables, a concern that others have noted in regard to some of the newer approaches,[1] and a criticism that Amos Wilder specifically raised in regard to my own work on the parables.

> I would qualify Hedrick's conjecture that the early church had lost touch with and forgotten the original meaning of Jesus' parables, with their context, and was thus impelled to seek such various readings of them. I would urge that their original force and bearing continued in a kind of underground way in the memory of the community.[2]

Wilder's concern is that my observations acutely raise "the problem of continuity in the literary tradition of the early church and also that of the linkage of the movement with its founder."[3] Wilder has seen the problem clearly enough, and argues that "these fictions have specific traits in their composition and vision which evoke a particular perspective, no doubt preconceptual, prepredicational and prenomistic, yet implicitly normative at that level."[4] He therefore excludes the idea that parables are "open to a gratuitous free play of signification."[5] But, alas, the history of parables interpretation, beginning with the canonical evangelists themselves, seems to prove him wrong. Parables have been, and still are, open to multiple ways of understanding them, and we do not seem able to close the gap between Jesus' intent and our multiple understandings.

In chapter 6 I noted certain objective features of the parables that limit the range and number of what I choose to call "plausible" readings. These constraints are part of the design of the parable. Therefore, I designate readings formulated within the limits of the constraints as "plausible" readings in the sense that they accord with the objective features of the parable. So in one sense I agree with Wilder; parables are not completely open to a "free play" of significations, because their design does not permit it. If interpretations violate the constraints placed on them by the design of the parable, they are simply implausible. Readings found to be plausible by the above criteria, however, are not to be construed as recovering the intention of Jesus, for there can be a range of plausible readings of the same parable. Because of their design, parables cannot be limited to only one reading.

Those who ponder the parables are custodians of secular narratives, which are characterized essentially by human immediacy—not divine immediacy, which is always brought to the parable as a particular reader's response. They do not "teach" anything in particular or in general; they do not provide normative guides for ethical human behavior; they do not reveal theological truths or overtly push any particular values—certainly not religious values. On the contrary, when read in historical context, it is in their nature to undermine paradigms, whether social, religious, or cultural. Indeed, in their secularity and amorality they have challenged religious paradigms for thoughtful readers since the first century. They raise questions and issues but provide no answers, and this is one reason the church, beginning with the canonical evangelists, has never been able to control them completely. The parables mean exactly what they say—and maybe more. But the "more" is what *readers* discover in the nexus between themselves and the parables; their discoveries are not actually *there* in the parables themselves. Readers provide the answers in response to the challenge of the parables. Readers entering their fictional worlds and engaging the narratives are rewarded not with answers to their questions but with challenges to their answers by having their cherished ideas, ideals, values, and faith undermined. As Frank Kermode said, "Fictions are for finding things out."[6]

Notes

For the abbreviations, see Patrick H. Alexander et al. eds., *The SBL Handbook of Style for Ancient Near Eastern, Biblical, and Early Christian Studies* (Peabody, Mass.: Hendrickson, 1999).

Preface

1. Northrop Frye, *Anatomy of Criticism: Four Essays* (Princeton, N.J.: Princeton University Press, 1957), 40.
2. Ibid., 41.

Introduction

1. W. O. E. Oesterley, *The Gospel Parables in the Light of Their Jewish Background* (London: S.P.C.K., 1936), 16.
2. Madeleine Boucher, *The Mysterious Parable: A Literary Study* (CBQMS 6; Washington, D.C.: CBA, 1977), 138–40.
3. Peter Rhea Jones, *The Teaching of the Parables* (Nashville: Broadman, 1982), 114–26.
4. David Wenham, *The Parables of Jesus* (Downers Grove, Ill.: InterVarsity, 1989), 197–98.
5. Bernard Brandon Scott, *Hear Then the Parable: A Commentary on the Parables of Jesus* (Minneapolis: Fortress, 1989), 334–38. For a discussion of the contradictory ways that parables are read see Charles W. Hedrick, "Prolegomena to Reading Parables: Luke 13:6–9 as a Test Case," *RevExp* 94, no. 2 (1997): 179–97.
6. Adolf Jülicher, *Die Gleichnisreden Jesu* (2 vols.; Leipzig: J. C. B. Mohr [Paul Siebeck], 1899), 1:300; Alexander Balman Bruce, *The Parabolic Teaching of Christ: A Systematic and Critical Study of the Parables of Our Lord* (3d rev. ed.; New York: Armstrong & Son, 1886 [1st ed., 1882]).
7. C. H. Dodd, *The Parables of the Kingdom* (New York: Charles Scribner's Sons, 1936), 16.

8. Dan Otto Via Jr., *The Parables: Their Literary and Existential Dimension* (Philadelphia: Fortress, 1967).
9. Charles W. Hedrick, *Parables as Poetic Fictions: The Creative Voice of Jesus* (Peabody, Mass.: Hendrickson, 1994).
10. William R. Herzog II, *Parables as Subversive Speech: Jesus as Pedagogue of the Oppressed* (Louisville, Ky.: Westminster John Knox, 1994), 3.
11. Joachim Jeremias, *The Parables of Jesus* (trans. S. H. Hooke; rev. ed.; New York: Charles Scribner's Sons, 1963), 132. According to Jeremias, the parable of the Prodigal Son/Elder Brother (Luke 15:11–32) "is primarily an apologetic parable, in which Jesus vindicates his table companionship with sinners against his critics" (ibid.), as Luke 15:1–3 indicates.
12. For a similar view of the state of scholarship on the parables—but from a very different perspective—see Craig L. Blomberg, "The Parables of Jesus: Current Trends and Needs in Research," in *Studying the Historical Jesus: Evaluations of Current Research* (ed. Bruce Chilton and Craig Evans; Leiden: E. J. Brill), 231–54; see his summary, 252–54.

Chapter One: What Is a Parable?

1. See Hedrick, *Parables as Poetic Fictions*, 13–16.
2. See John Dominic Crossan, *In Fragments: The Aphorisms of Jesus* (San Francisco: Harper & Row, 1983).
3. See Laurence Perrine, *Sound and Sense: An Introduction to Poetry* (5th ed.; New York: Harcourt Brace Jovanovich, 1977), 50–59.
4. Charles W. Hedrick, "The Thirty-Four Gospels," *BRev* 18, no. 3 (2000): 25–26.
5. See James M. Robinson, ed., *The Nag Hammadi Library in English* (3d completely rev. ed; San Francisco: Harper & Row, 1988), 1–26, 124–38. For another translation, see Robert J. Miller, ed., *The Complete Gospels: Annotated Scholars Version* (rev. and expanded ed.; Sonoma, Calif.: Polebridge, 1992), 301–29; and for the most recent discussion of the parables in Thomas, see Stevan Davies, *The Gospel of Thomas Annotated and Explained* (Woodstock, Vt.: Skylight Paths, 2002).
6. See Robinson, ed., *Nag Hammadi Library*, 29–37; and Miller, eds., *Complete Gospels*, 332–42. Citations to the text are from Miller.
7. See Charles W. Hedrick, "Kingdom Sayings and Parables of Jesus in the *Apocryphon of James:* Tradition and Redaction," *NTS* 29, no. 1 (1983): 9–13; and Ron Cameron, *Sayings Traditions in the Apocryphon of James* (HTS 34; Philadelphia: Fortress, 1984), 8–30.
8. The word *paroimia* is variously translated as "figure," "proverb," "maxim," "common saying," "comparison," and some New Testament translators even render it as "parable." In the New Testament, the word *paroimia* is only used in John (10:6; 16:25, 29), and once in 2 Pet 2:22, where its character as "proverb" is clear.
9. Compare also the contrast between private (secret) and open language in John: 7:4, 10, 13, 26; 11:54; 18:20. Figures are deliberately cloaked language.
10. For example, see Jeremias, *Parables of Jesus*, 197–98.
11. John Dominic Crossan, *Sayings Parallels: A Workbook for the Jesus Tradition* (Philadelphia: Fortress, 1986). Crossan lists it with the aphorisms (p. 69, no. 42). Brandon Scott does not discuss it in his *Hear Then the Parable.*
12. Adapted from Perrine, *Sound and Sense*, 81.
13. See the discussion in Norman Perrin, *Jesus and the Language of the Kingdom: Symbol and Metaphor in New Testament Interpretation* (Philadelphia: Fortress, 1976), 15–88, 194–205.

14. John Bunyan, *The Pilgrim's Progress from This World to That Which Is to Come Delivered under the Similitude of a Dream: Wherein Is Discovered the Manner of His Setting Out, His Dangerous Journey and Safe Arrival at the Desired Country* (London: J. & J. Cundee, 1811).
15. John Dominic Crossan, "Parable," in *The Anchor Bible Dictionary* (ed. David Noel Freedman; 6 vols.; New York: Doubleday, 1992), 5:148–50.
16. I am beginning to suspect that some of the sayings modern scholars call aphorisms are in all likelihood really proverbs. For example, the so-called twin images of the patched garment and wineskins in Matthew, Mark, and Luke sound like proverbial lore to my ear. Certainly they are good advice for first-century wine makers and seamstresses. They only appear odd when included among the sayings of a teacher of religion, and that may be why Luke thought they must have figurative character. Modern scholars follow Luke rather than Matthew and Mark, who do not seem to regard them as anything other than what they present themselves to be—good advice about making clothes and storing wine.

Chapter Two: Where to Begin?

1. See Jeremias, *Parables of Jesus*, 40.
2. Jeremias, *Parables of Jesus*, 11–114.
3. Jeremias, *Parables of Jesus*, 114. See pages 96–114 for his argument.
4. Scott, *Hear Then the Parable*, 76.
5. See Hedrick, *Parables as Poetic Fictions*, 17–28.
6. The failure of the *parousia* (the appearing of the Lord; i.e., his return) to occur immediately prompted a crisis in the early church that needed to be explained. Compare, for example, the imminent expectation of the early writings (1 Thess 4:13–18; 1 Cor 7:25–31) with expectations in a later writing (2 Pet 3:3–10).
7. See the discussion in Hedrick, *Parables as Poetic Fictions*, 187–207.
8. See Perrine, *Sound and Sense*, 136–40; John Ciardi, *How Does a Poem Mean?* (part 3 of *An Introduction to Literature*; Boston: Houghton Mifflin, 1959), 663–70; Emil Hurtik and Robert Yarber, *An Introduction to Poetry and Criticism* (Lexington, Mass.: Xerox College Publishing, 1972), 3–4.
9. See Hedrick, *Parables as Poetic Fictions*, 50–56, 78–87.
10. See the discussion in Via, *Parables*, 70–79. See also W. K. Wimsatt Jr. and M. C. Beardsley, "The Intentional Fallacy," *Sewanee Review* 54 (1946): 468–88; and the collection of essays on formal criticism in Donald Keesey, ed., *Contexts for Criticism* (3d ed.; Mountain View, Calif.: Mayfield, 1998), 71–138. The articles are: Donald Keesey, "Formal Criticism: Poem as Context," 71–79; Cleanth Brooks, "Irony as a Principle of Structure," 80–87; W. K. Wimsatt Jr., "The Structure of the Concrete Universal," 88–96; Mark Schorer, "Technique as Discovery," 97–107; Russ McDonald, "Reading *The Tempest*," 108–20; Helen Vendler, "Lional Trilling and the Immortality Ode," 121–32; John R. May, "Local Color in *The Awakening*," 133–38.
11. Amos N. Wilder, *Jesus' Parables and the War of Myths: Essays on Imagination in the Scriptures* (ed. James Breech; Philadelphia: Fortress, 1982), 89–90.
12. The subtle association between children and disciples is found in Matt 18:1–4, and is made more explicit in Matt 18:6: "One of these little ones who believe in me" is clearly a disciple.
13. See Miller, ed., *Complete Gospels*, 316.
14. Dodd, *Parables of the Kingdom*, 124–26.
15. See Charles W. Hedrick, "An Anecdotal Argument for the Independence of

the *Gospel of Thomas* from the Synoptic Gospels," in *For the Children, Perfect Instruction: Studies in Honor of Hans-Martin Schenke on the Occasion of the Berliner Arbeitskreis für koptisch-gnostische Schriften's Thirtieth Year* (ed. Hans-Gephard Bethge, Stephen Emmel, Karen L. King, and Imke Schletterer; Leiden: E. J. Brill, 2002), 113–16; and more fully in idem, "The Gospel of Thomas and Early Christian Tradition," in *Varia Gnostica* (ed. Marianne Aagaard Skovmand, Søren Giversen, and Jesper Hyldahl; Copenhagen: The Royal Danish Society of Sciences, Historical-Philosophical Information, forthcoming). See also Hedrick, *Parables as Poetic Fictions*, 236–51.

16. C. H. Roberts, *An Unpublished Fragment of the Fourth Gospel in the John Rylands Library* (Manchester: John Rylands Library, 1935), 16.
17. Ibid., 14–15.
18. See Hedrick, "Anecdotal Argument," 114–16.
19. See, for example, Craig L. Blomberg, *Interpreting the Parables* (Downers Grove, Ill.: InterVarsity Press, 1990), 179–84.
20. See, for example, Mary Ann Beavis, "The Foolish Landowner (Luke 12:16b–20)," in *Jesus and His Parables: Interpreting the Parables of Jesus Today* (ed. V. George Shillington; Edinburgh: T. & T. Clark, 1997), 57.
21. See, for example, Arland J. Hultgren, *The Parables of Jesus: A Commentary* (Grand Rapids: Eerdmans, 2000), 440–45. He also does not discuss the new parables in the *Secret Book of James.*
22. See, for example, Herzog, *Parables as Subversive Speech*, 83, 99–100.
23. See Charles W. Hedrick, "An Unfinished Story about a Fig Tree in a Vineyard (Luke 13:6–9)," *PRS* 26, no. 2 (Summer 1999): 169–72. This parable receives gnostic interpretations in *Pistis Sophia* and the *Apocalypse of Peter.*
24. See Blomberg, *Interpreting the Parables*, 29–69; and Brad H. Young, *The Parables: Jewish Tradition and Christian Interpretation* (Peabody, Mass.: Hendrickson, 1998), 3–38.
25. Lawrence H. Schiffman, *From Text to Tradition: A History of Second Temple Judaism* (Hoboken, N.J.: KTAV Publishing House, 1991), 187, 197; compare Mikeal C. Parsons, "The Critical Use of the Rabbinic Literature in New Testament Studies," *PRS* 12 (Summer 1985): 85–102, especially 90–92; and Scott, *Hear Then the Parable*, 14.
26. See Paul Fiebig, *Die Gleichnisreden Jesu im Lichte der rabbinischen Gleichnisse des neuen testamentlichen Zeitalters* (Tübingen: J. C. B. Mohr [Paul Siebeck], 1912), 1–118.
27. Scott, *Hear Then the Parable*, 44.
28. See Hedrick, *Parables as Poetic Fictions*, 254–55.
29. See Victor H. Matthews and Don C. Benjamin, eds., *Old Testament Parallels: Laws and Stories from the Ancient Near East* (rev. and expanded ed.; New York: Paulist Press, 1997). On p. 211 are two parables from a Middle Kingdom Egyptian text, "A Sufferer and a Soul in Egypt," which are quite similar to the parables of Jesus. On pp. 285–88 are three fables from an Assyrian text, "The Teachings of Ahiqar." I thank Victor Matthews for pointing out these parallels to me.
30. See Martin Hengel, *Judaism and Hellenism: Studies in Their Encounter in Palestine during the Early Hellenistic Period* (2 vols. in 1; trans. John Bowden; Philadelphia: Fortress, 1974).
31. See Mary Ann Beavis, "Parable and Fable," *CBQ* 52 (1990): 473–98.
32. See Ben Edwin Perry, *Babrius and Phaedrus: Newly Edited and Translated into English, together with an Historical Introduction and a Comprehensive Survey of*

Greek and Latin Fables in the Aesopic Tradition (Cambridge, Mass.: Harvard University Press, 1984), xi–xiv. In fact, the earliest extant manuscript of a collection of Aesop's fables is dated to the mid-second century (p. lxx), relatively the same date as the earliest extant gospel manuscripts: a fragment of the Gospel of John, and Papyrus Egerton 2.

33. Perry, *Babrius and Phaedrus*, lix–lxi, lxxxiv–xc.
34. Ibid., xxi–xxiii.
35. Ibid., xiv–xvi.
36. Ibid., 258–59 (Phaedrus book 3, no. 1).
37. Ibid., 32–35 (Babrius, no. 22). The *epimythium* is bracketed because Perry does not regard it as an original conclusion. In any case, none of the *epimythia* are thought to be original endings to the story; see pp. lxii–lxiii.
38. Ben Edwin Perry, *Aesopica: A Series of Texts relating to Aesop or Ascribed to Him or Closely Connected with the Literary Tradition That Bears His Name. Collected and Critically Edited, in Part Translated from Oriental Languages with a Commentary and Historical Essay*, vol. 1, *Greek and Latin Texts* (Urbana, Ill.: University of Illinois Press, 1952), no. 178 (the translation of the moral is my own); the rest of the translation is by Perry, *Babrius and Phaedrus*, 455, no. 178.
39. For the Greek text, see Perry, *Aesopica*, no. 204 (the translation of the moral is my own); the rest of the translation is by Perry, *Babrius and Phaedrus*, 461, no. 204.
40. Of course, by comparing different versions of the fable, if they exist, it is possible to see the same attempts at improving the story as are found with the parables of Jesus in the canonical gospels. For example, there is another version of the Tanner and the Rich Man in which the tanner "tells the rich man that he will get used to the bad smells in a short time, but the rich man is unwilling to lose his sense of smell for the benefit of the tanner's trade." Perry, *Babrius and Phaedrus*, 461; see also the discussion on pp. xlii–xliii.
41. See Perry, *Babrius and Phaedrus*, 597, no. 702.
42. Perry, *Babrius and Phaedrus*, 9–10, no. 4.
43. For a different interpretation of the evidence, see Scott, *Hear Then the Parable*, 313–16.
44. Contrary to what might be expected, the comparison is not always with the kingdom of God/heaven. Parables are also compared to one who hears and does Jesus' words, the return of the Son of Man, and the Man (*Thom* 8). See Hedrick, *Parables as Poetic Fictions*, 258.
45. See Charles W. Hedrick, "Parable and Kingdom: A Survey of the Evidence in Mark," *PRS* 27, no. 2 (Summer 2000): 193–96; and idem, *Parables as Poetic Fictions*, 26–28. To judge from the multiple interpretations (Luke 16:8–12) of the parable of the Dishonest Steward (Luke 16:1–7), some parables at least were problems for Christian interpreters. The "conclusions" in Luke 16:8–12 appear only in Luke and for that reason were most likely connected to the parable in its period of oral transmission rather than by Luke. Luke 16:13 is Luke's own interpretation, taken from the hypothetical sayings gospel Q, and added at the end of the traditional string of interpretations.
46. See Hedrick, "Parable and Kingdom," 179–99, for the evidence.
47. See Hedrick, *Parables as Poetic Fictions*, 254–55. These calculations count every version of a parable as a separate instance.
48. In only two instances is there a problem. The parables of the Feast (Matt 22:1–10 = Luke 14:16–23) and the Entrusted Money (Matt 25:14–28 = Luke 19:12–24) disagree on the comparative frames. In both instances

Matthew has comparative frames and Luke does not. All the other Q parables and common synoptic parables agree on including or excluding the comparative frame.

49. See Scott's treatment of the parable of the Samaritan (Luke 10:30–35), *Hear Then the Parable*, 189–202, and his rationale, 35–62.
50. See Blomberg's treatment of the Lost Sheep (Luke 15:4–7 = Matt 18:12–14) and the Lost Coin (Luke 15:8–10), *Interpreting the Parables*, 179–84, and his rationale, 29–69.
51. See Via's treatment of the parable of the Ten Maidens (Matt 25:12), *Parables*, 122–128, and his rationale, 70–107.
52. See Hultgren, *Parables of Jesus*, 169–79.
53. See Madeleine I. Boucher, *The Parables* (rev. ed.; New Testament Message 7; Wilmington, Del.: Michael Glazier, 1983), 120–25.

Chapter Three: Is Jesus Really the Author of the Parables?

1. To see why someone would think Jesus did not originate all the parables see Robert W. Funk, Bernard Brandon Scott, and James R. Butts, *The Parables of Jesus: Red Letter Edition. A Report of the Jesus Seminar* (Sonoma, Calif.: Polebridge, 1988).
2. By "historical man" I mean Jesus as he can be reconstructed on the basis of modern historical methodology.
3. See the dates given to the list of New Testament manuscripts in Eberhard Nestle, Erwin Nestle, Barbara Aland, and Kurt Aland, eds., *Greek-English New Testament* (Stuttgart: Deutsche Bibelgesellschaft, 1998), 684–718. The earliest complete versions of the gospels are found in manuscripts of the fourth century.
4. See Josephus, *Jewish War*, 6.220–87 (*Josephus: The Jewish War* [trans. H. St. J. Thackery; 8 vols.; New York: Putnam, 1928], 439–59). Note that in *Jewish War*, 7.1 (Thackery, 3:504–5), while the temple was destroyed by fire, Caesar gave the order to raze the building to the ground. Today all that is left are some foundation stones known as the "wailing wall."
5. See, for example, E. P. Sanders and Margaret Davies, *Studying the Synoptic Gospels* (Philadelphia: Trinity Press International, 1989), 16–21.
6. Werner Georg Kümmel, *Introduction to the New Testament* (trans. Howard C. Kee; 17th ed.; Nashville: Abingdon, 1975), 482–83; and Helmut Koester, "The Text of the Synoptic Gospels in the Second Century," in *Gospel Traditions in the Second Century: Origins, Recensions, Texts, and Transmission* (ed. William L. Petersen; Notre Dame, Ind.: University of Notre Dame Press, 1989), 26–28. See the study by William Sanday, *The Gospels in the Second Century: An Examination of the Critical Part of a Work Entitled "Supernatural Religion"* (London: Macmillan, 1876), 310–15.
7. See Charles W. Hedrick, *When History and Faith Collide: Studying Jesus* (Peabody, Mass.; Hendrickson, 1999), 76–94.
8. The Gospel of John is a special problem, and there is no consensus on whether or not John used Mark as a source.
9. This date is based on the fact that Pontius Pilate was prefect of Judea from 26 to 36 C.E. and on Luke's observation (Luke 3:23) that Jesus was around thirty years of age when he began his public career.
10. See Hedrick, *When History and Faith Collide*, 110–25.
11. See Hedrick, *When History and Faith Collide*, 48–75.

12. See, for example, the different "profiles" of Jesus in Roy W. Hoover, ed., *Profiles of Jesus* (Santa Rosa, Calif.: Polebridge, 2002).
13. See the collection of articles in Keesey, ed., *Contexts for Criticism*, 9–70 (the author as context for interpretation), and 71–138 (the poem as context for interpretation). The articles are: (the author as context for interpretation) Donald Keesey, "Historical Criticism I: Author as Context," 9–16; E. D. Hirsch Jr., "Objective Interpretation," 17–28; George Watson, "Are Poems Historical Acts?" 29–33; Alastair Fowler, "Intention Floreat," 34–39; Paul Yachnin, "Shakespere and the Idea of Obedience: Gonzalo in *The Tempest*," 40–52; Daniel W. Ross, "Seeking a Way Home: The Uncanny in Wordsworth's Immortality Ode," 53–64; (the poem as context for interpretation) see chap. 2, note 10 for a listing of the articles discussing the poem as context. See also Via, *Parables*, 70–107. Via applies these insights to the parables.
14. Wallace Stevens to Hi Simons 9 January 1940, in *Letters of Wallace Stevens* (ed. Holly Stevens; New York: Alfred A. Knopf, 1966), 346.

Chapter Four: Why Did Jesus Speak in Parables?

1. See Via, *Parables*, 12.
2. See Robert H. Stein, *An Introduction to the Parables of Jesus* (Philadelphia: Westminster, 1981), 20. Stein gives a list of parables he takes to be example stories.
3. M. C. Howatson, *The Oxford Companion to Classical Literature* (2d ed.; New York: Oxford University Press, 1989), 487. See John Henry Freese, *Aristotle: The "Art" of Rhetoric* (Cambridge, Mass.: Harvard University Press, 1947), 14–15; Aristotle, *Rhet.* 1.2.
4. Aristotle, *Rhet.* 2.20.2–3.
5. Ibid., 2.20.3–4.
6. Modern scholars of the parables of Jesus apply the word "metaphor" to the entire story Jesus told. Aristotle, on the other hand, uses the word "metaphor" (*metaphora*) in connection with his discussion of "poetry," which refers to the work of dramatists and epic poets (Aristotle, *Poet.* 1.1–6). Metaphor is the use of a word or phrase, normally applicable for something in one context, applied to a different thing in a different context. The "poet" sees a connection between the items and *by analogy* brings the one over applying it to the other (Aristotle, *Poet.* 21.7–26); see W. Hamilton Fyfe and W. Rhys Roberts, *Aristotle, The Poetics; Longinus, On the Sublime; Demetrius, On Style* (Cambridge, Mass.: Harvard University Press, 1953), 5–9, 81–85.
7. See A. M. Harmon, *Lucian with an English Translation* (New York, Macmillan, 1913), 1.vii.
8. He even uses Aesop's fables, originally intended for more serious ends, in his humor. See Harmon, *Lucian*, 5:70–71, 380–81.
9. James R. Butts, "The Progymnasmata of Theon: A New Text with Translation and Commentary" (Ph.D. diss., Claremont Graduate School, 1986), 259.
10. Butts, "Progymnasmata of Theon," 279.
11. Perry, *Babrius and Phaedrus*, 190–91; see also 232–33, and 254–55.
12. See the discussion about dating the sources in chapter 3.
13. See the discussion in chapter 6.
14. See *Thom* 1: "Whoever finds the interpretation of these words will not taste death."

15. Harold W. Attridge, *Nag Hammadi Codex I (The Jung Codex): Introductions, Texts, Translations, Indices* (NHS 22–23; Leiden: E. J. Brill, 1985), 39.
16. All three texts provide allegorical interpretations to the parable of the Sower, but Matthew also includes allegorical interpretations to the Weeds in the Field (Matt 13:36–43) and the Seine Net (13:47–50).
17. Matthew 13:14–15 stands in tension with Matt 13:11. In 13:11 the secrets are deliberately concealed from the crowd, but in 13:14–15 the crowd does not understand because of their own hardness of heart.
18. On the basis of the current understanding of relationships among the Synoptic Gospels, Matthew used Mark as a source. Thus, with regard to the material shared by Matthew and Mark, Matthew's version represents a later editing of Mark.
19. One exception may be Blomberg, *Interpreting the Parables*, 53–55.
20. See, for example, William L. Lane, *The Gospel according to Mark* (NICNT 2; Grand Rapids: Eerdmans, 1974), 156–59; and Vincent Taylor, *The Gospel according to St. Mark* (New York: Macmillan, 1959), 254–55.
21. See Charles E. Carlston, *The Parables of the Triple Tradition* (Philadelphia: Fortress, 1975), 101; Jeremias, *Parables of Jesus*, 15; Hultgren, *Parables of Jesus*, 453–57.
22. See, for example, Stein, *Introduction to the Parables of Jesus*, 27–35.
23. See Carlston, *Parables of the Triple Tradition*, 97.
24. See Jeremias, *Parables of Jesus*, 66–89, for the definitive proof of this point.
25. See, for example, Hedrick, *Parables as Poetic Fictions*, 164–86 (the Sower); and Herzog, *Parables as Subversive Speech*, 79–97 (Laborers in the Vineyard).

Chapter Five: What Do Parables Present to the Reader?

1. See Dale B. Martin, "Social-Scientific Criticism," in *To Each Its Own Meaning: An Introduction to Biblical Criticisms and their Application* (ed. Steven L. McKenzie and Stephen R. Haynes; rev. and expanded ed.; Louisville, Ky.: Westminster John Knox, 1999), 125–41.
2. Martin, "Social-Scientific Criticism," 125.
3. This is Norman Perrin's evaluation of Jülicher's history of parables interpretation in *Gleichnisreden Jesu*, 1:203–322 (Perrin, *Language of the Kingdom*, 93); see Dodd's evaluation of Jülicher (Dodd, *Parables of the Kingdom*, 24, 112); note that Jeremias also appreciates the realism of the parables (Jeremias, *Parables of Jesus*, 11–12, 19).
4. Dodd, *Parables of the Kingdom*, 16, cf. 24, 112.
5. Jeremias, *Parables of Jesus*, 11.
6. See Jeremias, *Parables of Jesus*, 66–96.
7. Amos N. Wilder, *Early Christian Rhetoric: The Language of the Gospel* (Peabody, Mass.: Hendrickson, 1999), 73.
8. Perrin, *Language of the Kingdom*, 104.
9. Ibid., 105.
10. M. H. Abrams, *A Glossary of Literary Terms* (6th ed.; Fort Worth: Harcourt Brace, 1993), 4. The material quoted is Abrams's definition of allegory.
11. This theory is from Scott, *Hear Then the Parable*, 18.
12. There are exceptions where parables shade over into unrealism, however.
13. Scott, *Hear Then the Parable*, viii–ix.
14. Hedrick, *Parables as Poetic Fictions*, 259–61.
15. See the discussion in Scott, *Hear Then the Parable*, 103–5.

16. See for example, Jeremias, *Parables of Jesus*, 128–32; and Hultgren, *Parables of Jesus*, 86–87.
17. See, for example, Scott, *Hear Then the Parable*, 108–22; Richard Q. Ford, *The Parables of Jesus: Recovering the Art of Listening* (Minneapolis: Fortress, 1997), 90–106; and James Breech, *The Silence of Jesus: The Authentic Voice of the Historical Man* (Philadelphia: Fortress, 1983), 186–212.
18. Jeremias, however, regards this particular setting as a genuine bit of history from the public career of Jesus (*Parables of Jesus*, 131–32).
19. See the insightful essay by Richard L. Rohrbaugh, "A Dysfunctional Family and Its Neighbors (Luke 15:11b–32)," in *Jesus and His Parables: Interpreting the Parables of Jesus Today* (ed. V. George Shillington; Edinburgh: T. & T. Clark, 1997), 141–64.
20. These are not slaves but rather people hired (*misthos*) for work.
21. The son asked for his share of the property (*ousia*) but the father divided up his "livelihood" (*bios*). To what extent this may be pressed is not clear; what is clear is that the narrator has made a distinction. So it is at least possible that the father did not give the younger son real estate but simply the equivalent of what was due him in liquid form. This distinction makes the father appear less foolish, as Rohrbaugh suggests in "Dysfunctional Family," 164.
22. The younger son's share is usually described as one-third (Deut 21:15–17; cf. Gen 25:29–34 on the right of primogeniture).
23. The father had enough control over the family assets to give the returning son the "best" robe the family had (15:22) and to throw a party for the son with the neighbors, all without consulting the older son (15:23).
24. See, for example, Scott, *Hear Then the Parable*, 117.
25. Scott, *Hear Then the Parable*, 117.
26. Sirach 33:19–21 advises against giving property to children before the owner dies. The admonition not to do it suggests that such transference of property to children did happen before the death of the parent-owner, but as Scott avers, "it is surely not the norm" (111). See Scott's discussion of this point and the other parallels he lists in *Hear Then the Parable*, 109–11.
27. See 15:26. The word used here is *pais*, not *doulos*.
28. Kenneth E. Bailey, *Poet and Peasant and Through Peasant Eyes* (2 vols. in 1; Grand Rapids: Eerdmans, 1976), 194–95, followed with some hesitation by Rohrbaugh, "Dysfunctional Family," 159–60. Rohrbaugh, however, reads the incident as an insult to the father.
29. The fact that the father talks down to the older son, calling him "child" (*teknon*, 15:31) rather than "son" (*huios*), probably didn't help his disposition, either. Apparently the father still treated him as a subordinate rather than as a master of the house. The property had been divided (15:12) and the younger was master of his share (15:13), but the older apparently did not control the share he had been given. The older son's share was still controlled by the father (15:31: "all that is mine is yours").
30. Rohrbaugh argues that the older brother's harsh words about the younger son's behavior in the far country (15:30) are simply not true. At the very least, however, they do signal the break between the brothers.
31. See Herzog, *Parables as Subversive Speech*, 79–97.
32. Herzog, *Parables as Subversive Speech*, 92.
33. Hedrick, *Parables as Poetic Fictions*, 172–73.
34. See Hedrick, "Unfinished Story about a Fig Tree," 178–84.

Chapter Six: What Does a Parable Mean?

1. Stein, *Introduction to the Parables of Jesus*, 122–23.
2. Scott, *Hear Then the Parable*, 75.
3. *The Random House College Dictionary*, rev. ed. (1975).
4. See Meier Sternberg, *The Poetics of Biblical Narrative: Ideological Literature and the Drama of Reading* (Bloomington, Ind.: Indiana University Press, 1987), 186–229; idem, *Expositional Modes and Temporal Ordering in Fiction* (Baltimore: Johns Hopkins University Press, 1978), 50–53, 38–246; and Wolfgang Iser, *The Act of Reading: A Theory of Aesthetic Response* (Baltimore: Johns Hopkins University Press, 1978), 163–70, 182–203.
5. Scott, *Hear Then the Parable*, 120.
6. Eta Linnemann, *Jesus of the Parables: Introduction and Exposition* (trans. John Sturdy; New York: Harper & Row, 1966), 10, 79.
7. Ibid., 79. Those who are persuaded by Linnemann are Scott, *Hear Then the Parable*, 119; Bailey, *Poet and Peasant*, 192; Rohrbaugh, "Dysfunctional Family," 158–59. Hultgren does not cite Linnemann, but seems to agree with her idea (Hultgren, *Parables of Jesus*, 80). On the other hand, Peter Rhea Jones, *Studying the Parables of Jesus* (Macon, Ga.: Smith & Helwys, 1999), 219; and John R. Donahue, *The Gospel in Parable: Metaphor, Narrative, and Theology in the Synoptic Gospels* (Philadelphia: Fortress, 1988), 156, do not mind the gap.
8. See Breech, *Silence of Jesus*, 199 ("apparently he [i.e., the father] has forgotten about his elder son's existence"), and 203–4, for yet a third way of understanding the reason for the elder son's anger: "He is angry *because the father does not care about himself*" (204), apparently because he lets the younger son take advantage of him.
9. See the discussion in chapter 2.
10. See the comments in chapter 3.
11. The term derives from the New Criticism focus on the "form" of the artistic work. See the brief discussion in Wilfred L. Guerin, Earle Labor, Lee Morgan, Jeanne C. Reesman, and John R. Willingham, *A Handbook of Critical Approaches to Literature* (3d ed.; New York: Oxford University Press, 1992), 62–115.
12. Guerin et al., *Handbook of Critical Approaches*, 98. When one considers the rather limited number of parables that are to be found in Greco-Roman antiquity, the parables of Jesus would clearly qualify as an art form. They are certainly brief fictions.
13. R. W. Stallman, "Intentions, problem of," in *Princeton Encyclopedia of Poetry and Poetics* (ed. Alex Preminger, Frank J. Warnke, and O. B. Hardison Jr.; enlarged ed.; Princeton, N.J.: Princeton University Press, 1974), 398.
14. See the brief evaluation in Guerin et al., *Handbook of Critical Approaches*, 114–15.
15. Stallman, "Intentions, problem of," 399.
16. See chapter 3.
17. Samuel Hazo, "Affective Fallacy," in Preminger et al., eds., *Princeton Encyclopedia of Poetry*, 8.
18. Charles W. Hedrick, "The Lion's Tooth," *Shiftless Stone Review* 1 (1991): 2. The poem was published under the English title. Used with permission.
19. The very poor would not see dandelion season as a struggle for lawn "acceptability," but would treat the dandelion as a food source (i.e., dandelion wine, tea, and salad). The very rich would have a handyman to worry with such

things. It would only be a personal struggle for those bound by middle-class incomes and values.

20. C. F. Main and Peter J. Seng, *Poems* (2d ed.; Belmont, Calif.: Wadsworth, 1965), 23; X. J. Kennedy, *An Introduction to Poetry* (Boston: Little, Brown & Co., 1966), 2–5; Ciardi, *How Does a Poem Mean?* 667–70; Perrine, *Sound and Sense*, 27–28.
21. Perrine, *Sound and Sense*, 4.
22. See Martin Steinmann Jr., "Heresy of Paraphrase," in Preminger et al., eds., *Princeton Encyclopedia of Poetry*, 344–45.

Chapter Seven: Jesus the Figure Maker

1. C. Hugh Holman and William Harmon, *A Handbook to Literature* (5th ed.; New York: Macmillan, 1986), 202–3.
2. See the discussion of the literary types scholars have found in the parables, including the three covered in this chapter, in chapter 1.
3. See the introduction.
4. Compare, for example, the strange and different readings of Jesus' realistic story about robbery and assault on the road to Jericho (Luke 10:30–35) by Augustine (given briefly in Dodd, *Parables of the Kingdom*, 1–20) and by Richard C. Trench, *Notes on the Parables of Our Lord* (London: Pickering & Inglis, 1953), 311–28.
5. See, for example, Matthew's interpretation of the Weeds in the Field: Matt 13:24–30, 36–43.
6. See, for example, Hultgren, *Parables of Jesus*, 12–14; and Donahue, *Gospel in Parable*, 11–12.
7. For a sympathetic treatment of the allegorical method, see Mikeal C. Parsons, "'Allegorizing Allegory': Narrative Analysis and Parable Interpretation," *PRS* 15, no. 2 (1988): 147–64.
8. Blomberg, *Interpreting the Parables*, 29–69; see also his "Interpreting the Parables of Jesus: Where Are We and Where Do We Go from Here?" *CBQ* 53 (1991): 50–78.
9. Blomberg, *Interpreting the Parables*, 16.
10. Ibid., 20.
11. Ibid., 21.
12. Ibid.
13. Ibid., 19–20. He also accepts the Markan messianic secret as a historical circumstance in the life of Jesus, and links this motif to the parables as further proof of Jesus' use of allegory (pp. 39–40).
14. See Blomberg, *Interpreting the Parables*, 58–69; compare the discussion in Hedrick, "Parable and Kingdom," 179–99.
15. Blomberg, *Interpreting the Parables*, 21.
16. Ibid., 61–65.
17. He is well aware that the extant versions of the rabbinic parables are considerably later than the time of Jesus (second century and later): Blomberg, *Interpreting the Parables*, 49, 58.
18. Blomberg, *Interpreting the Parables*, 268–71.
19. Ibid., 268, cf. 248.
20. Ibid., 51. Blomberg doesn't quite know what to do with the vinedresser, as well as certain other elements in the story. He only knows what the vinedresser is not to be equated with, namely, Jesus.
21. Hedrick, "Unfinished Story about a Fig Tree," 186–89.

22. Blomberg, *Interpreting the Parables*, 49–50. There is a difference between reference and inference. Blomberg writes: "a cross . . . might appear as an entirely natural element in the story line of a given piece of fiction, while at the same time *evoking* memories of the crucifixion of Jesus" (p. 50; italics mine). In Blomberg's statement, the cross in the story is neutral, but for certain readers who bring the right baggage to the narrative, it evokes the cross of Jesus and in some cases leads them to the inference that the story actually *intends* to evoke the cross of Jesus.
23. Ibid., 269. He does not want to stumble out of orthodoxy into the "Marcionite heresy."
24. See Hedrick, "Prolegomena to Reading Parables," 181–90.
25. Boucher, *Parables*, 30.
26. This is contrary to Boucher, *Parables*, 30–31; and Blomberg, *Interpreting the Parables*, 43.
27. Dodd, *Parables of the Kingdom*, 5–6.
28. See Robert W. Funk, "How Do You Read? (Luke 10:25–37)," *Int* 18 (1964): 56–61; and idem, "The Good Samaritan as Metaphor," in *Parables and Presence: Forms of the New Testament Tradition* (Philadelphia: Fortress, 1982), 74–81. His argument for parables as metaphor is set forth in *Language, Hermeneutic, and Word of God* (New York: Harper & Row, 1966), 133–62.
29. See John Dominic Crossan, *In Parables: The Challenge of the Historical Jesus* (New York: Harper & Row, 1973).
30. Crossan, *In Parables*, 14.
31. Ibid., 13.
32. See Scott, *Hear Then the Parable*, 56–62.
33. Crossan, *In Parables*, 32.
34. Or as Amos Wilder puts it: "[A] true metaphor or symbol is more than a sign, it is a bearer of the reality to which it refers. The hearer not only learns about that reality, he participates in it. He is invaded by it." Wilder, *The Language of the Gospel: Early Christian Rhetoric* (New York: Harper & Row, 1964), 92. See also Funk, *Language, Hermeneutic, and Word of God*, 140.
35. Crossan, *In Parables*, 23; Scott, *Hear Then the Parable*, 61–62.
36. See Hedrick, "Parable and Kingdom," esp. 191–96.
37. See Hedrick, "Parable and the Kingdom," 182–88.
38. Robert Francis, "The Hound," in Perrine, *Sound and Sense*, 62. Used with permission.
39. Robert Frost, "Bereft," in Perrine, *Sound and Sense*, 62.
40. See Hedrick, *Parables as Poetic Fictions*, 28–32.
41. See Scott, *Hear Then the Parable*, 331–38.
42. See Scott, *Hear Then the Parable*, 76, 21–30.
43. Scott, *Hear Then the Parable*, 8; for symbol, see the discussion later in this chapter.
44. See Scott, *Hear Then the Parable*, 334–35, where Scott notes the meaning of the parable in Luke's context (see also his discussion on p. 75).
45. Scott, *Hear Then the Parable*, 332; see his discussion on 332–34.
46. Scott, *Hear Then the Parable*, 336–37. Scott and Blomberg are actually working at different levels, however: Blomberg considers the plausibility of exploiting these features as allegorical hooks but does not use them, and Scott considers the features significant for understanding the story.
47. "If it bears fruit in the coming . . ." What is missing is a statement about what the owner will do if the tree bears fruit. Most translators of Luke restore the

apodosis, with a translation that assumes the owner will let it live, since that seems to be implied by the second half of the statement: "if [it does] not [bear fruit], you will cut it down." Since translators fill in the ellipsis in their translations, most English readers are not even aware anything is missing from the text.

48. Scott, *Hear Then the Parable*, 338.
49. Funk, "Good Samaritan as Metaphor," 34.
50. Ibid.
51. Crossan, *In Parables*, 65.
52. Perrin, *Language of the Kingdom*, 33; see his discussion on 29–30.
53. Ibid., 203.
54. See the brief discussion in Perrine, *Sound and Sense*, 80–88.
55. Perrine, *Sound and Sense*, 83.
56. See Holman and Harmon, *Handbook to Literature*, 494; and Abrams, *Glossary of Literary Terms*, 206–8. For examples, see the discussion in Perrine, *Sound and Sense*, 80–88.
57. Samuel Taylor Coleridge, as quoted in Holman and Harmon, *Handbook to Literature*, 494.
58. Crossan, *In Parables*, 66.
59. See James M. Robinson, "Jesus' Parables as God Happening," in *A Meeting of Poets and Theologians to Discuss Parable, Myth, and Language* (ed. Tony Stoneburner; Cambridge, Mass.: Church Society for College Work, 1968), 45–52.
60. See Scott's discussion of the fig tree in Hebrew literature, *Hear Then the Parable*, 332–34; and the discussion in Hedrick, "Unfinished Story about a Fig Tree," 186–87.

Chapter Eight: Jesus the Ethicist

1. Herzog, *Parables as Subversive Speech*, 3.
2. Jeremias, *Parables of Jesus*, 19.
3. See Jülicher, *Gleichnisreden Jesu*, 1.203–25.
4. Jülicher, *Gleichnisreden Jesu*, 1:321–22; see also Perrin, *Language of the Kingdom*, 93.
5. Jülicher, *Gleichnisreden Jesu*, 1:322.
6. Ibid.
7. Jeremias, *Parables of Jesus*, 18; "It is well known that we owe to A. Jülicher the final discarding of the allegorical method of interpretation. It is positively alarming to read in his [book] the story of the centuries of distortion and ill-usage which the parables have suffered through allegorical interpretation." Also quoted by Perrin, *Language of the Kingdom*, 93.
8. See the argument for a limited allegory by Blamberg in chapter 7.
9. See Jülicher, *Gleichnisreden Jesu*, 1:52–58.
10. Jülicher, *Gleichnisreden Jesu*, 1:58, 117.
11. See the table of contents in vol. 2 of Jülicher, *Gleichnisreden Jesu.*
12. Jülicher, *Gleichnisreden Jesu*, 1:49, 117. The four example stories are the Pharisee and the Toll Collector (Luke 18:9–14), the Rich Man and Lazarus (Luke 16:19–31), the Rich Fool (Luke 12:16–20), and the Good Samaritan (Luke 10:30–37).
13. See Jülicher, *Gleichnisreden Jesu*, 1:69–80.
14. Jülicher, *Gleichnisreden Jesu*, 1:83.
15. Ibid., 1:70. Samples of Jülicher's general morals can be found in Jeremias, *Parables of Jesus*, 19.

16. Jülicher, *Gleichnisreden Jesu*, 2:585.
17. Ibid., 2:596. For examples of what others have found, see Jeremias, *Parables of Jesus*, 19; Perrin, *Language of the Kingdom*, 96–97; Stein, *Introduction to the Parables of Jesus*, 55.
18. See Jülicher, *Gleichnisreden Jesu*, 2:433–48.
19. Jülicher, *Gleichnisreden Jesu*, 2:441.
20. Ibid., 2:443.
21. Ibid.
22. Hedrick, "Prolegomena to Reading Parables," 181.
23. Hedrick, "Unfinished Story about a Fig Tree," 187, 189–90.
24. Perrin, *Language of the Kingdom*, 96.
25. Jones, *Studying the Parables of Jesus*, 3. But it should be noted that eschatology is not found in the parables either. Like Jülicher's morals, eschatology must also be imported into the parable by the reader.
26. Perrin, *Language of the Kingdom*, 95.
27. See the discussion of this point in Hedrick, "Unfinished Story about a Fig Tree," 186–92.
28. Herzog, *Parables as Subversive Speech*, 1.
29. Ibid., 1–2.
30. Ibid., 3.
31. Ibid., 50.
32. Ibid., 9.
33. Ibid., 27.
34. Ibid., 9.
35. Ibid., 17–19.
36. Ibid., 22.
37. Ibid., 23.
38. Ibid., 19–20.
39. Ibid., 23.
40. Ibid., 20–21.
41. Ibid., 21.
42. Ibid., 22.
43. Freire as quoted by Herzog, *Parables as Subversive Speech*, 22. It is called "conscientization" because "it defined a movement from a dominated consciousness to a critically active consciousness" (p. 24).
44. Herzog, *Parables as Subversive Speech*, 22.
45. Ibid., 16–17.
46. Ibid., 25–27.
47. See Herzog's discussion of the nature of agrarian societies in *Parables as Subversive Speech*, 53–73.
48. Herzog, *Parables as Subversive Speech*, 26.
49. Ibid., 27–28.
50. See Stein's criticism of Jülicher, for example, in Stein, *Introduction to the Parables of Jesus*, 55–56.
51. Why Jesus was crucified, of course, depends a great deal on the context. As one reviewer has pointed out, some years after Jesus "Pliny junior could execute Christians proclaiming a commendable morality merely for their obstinacy (*Letters*, 10.96)." F. Gerald Downing, review of W. R. Herzog II, *Parables as Subversive Speech*, *Theology* 98 (1995): 387.
52. Ibid., 77–97.

53. Ibid., 77.
54. Ibid., 79–80.
55. Ibid., 82.
56. This ending has been challenged; see Herzog, *Parables as Subversive Speech*, 82–83 for the sources. Matthew 20:8c has also been challenged as a Matthean addition, but Herzog takes the order of payment as central to the parable (p. 83).
57. Herzog, *Parables as Subversive Speech*, 85.
58. Ibid., 86.
59. Ibid., 87.
60. Ibid., 89–90.
61. Ibid., 90.
62. Ibid., 91–92.
63. Ibid., 92.
64. Ibid., 95.
65. See the reviews of *Parables as Subversive Speech* by John Dominic Crossan, *BTB* 25, no. 3 (1995): 145; Downing, *Theology* 98 (1995): 386–87; Paul Priest, *HBT* 18, no. 1 (1996): 110–11; Barbara E. Reid, *CBQ* 58 (1996): 348–49.
66. Not all are willing to concede even that, however. Craig Blomberg argues that Herzog's economic applications are challenged by the fact that an economic emphasis was never caught up in the later Jesus tradition. Blomberg, "Poetic Fictions, Subversive Speech, and Proportional Analogy in the Parables: Are We Making Any Progress in Parable Research?" *HBT* 18, no. 1 (1996): 122; see also his review of Herzog in *CRBR* 8 (1995): 227–29.
67. A Mustard Seed (Mark 4:31–32; Matt 13:31b–32; Luke 13:19; *Thom* 20), a Sprouting Seed (Mark 4:26–29; *Thom* 21d), the Ear of Grain (*Sec. Book Jas.* 12:22–27), the Date Palm Shoot (*Sec. Book Jas.* 7:22–27), A Sower (Mark 4:3–8; Matt 13:3b–8; Luke 8:5–8a; *Thom* 9).
68. Such as, for example, a Fig Tree in a Vineyard. See the classification in Hedrick, *Parables as Poetic Fictions*, 259–61; the texts are given on pp. 252–53.
69. Luke Timothy Johnson, review of W. R. Herzog II, *Parables as Subversive Speech*, *TS* 56, no. 3 (1995): 571–72.
70. There are problems with all theories that try to explain Jesus in terms of one issue.
71. Crossan notes this is his (positive) review of Herzog: Jesus could not control "how the audience could, would, should, react to the story." Crossan, review of Herzog, 144.
72. Herzog, *Parables as Subversive Speech*, 95: "It is probably impossible to reconstruct the lively conversation that the encoded parable generated" (noted also by Crossan).
73. See chapter 6.

Chapter Nine: Jesus the Existentialist and Bard

1. Via, *Parables*, 96.
2. Ibid., 96–101.
3. Ibid., 88–93.
4. Ibid., 25.
5. Ibid., 87. Via, however, does not completely reject the idea that parables reference something beyond themselves. Readers "will be subsidiarily aware—aware at lower levels of consciousness of various kinds of pointing outward to

the world outside the narrative," he says (p. 87), but this is not the same as saying that parables deliberately reference some other specific reality outside of themselves. These "lower levels of consciousness" to which he refers are what the parable "evokes" in certain readers, and evoking is not the same as deliberately referencing. See chapter 6.

6. Via does not completely reject the historical circumstances of the author (p. 93), but the author's circumstances are clearly not of any major significance for the way Via treats the parables (p. 95). See Hedrick, *Parables as Poetic Fictions*, 79–80.
7. Via, *Parables*, 77. Via draws heavily on the insights of the so-called New Criticism. In this citation, he is quoting from two leading proponents of the New Criticism, namely, William K. Wimsatt and Monroe C. Beardsley. See chapter 6 for a brief discussion of the New Criticism.
8. These are discussed in chapter 6.
9. Via, *Parables*, 77–78.
10. Ibid., 37.
11. Ibid., 39.
12. Ibid., 40.
13. Günther Bornkamm, *Jesus of Nazareth* (trans. Irene and Fraser Mcluskey with James M. Robinson; London: Hodder & Stoughton, 1960), 70; quoted in Via, *Parables*, 22.
14. Via, *Parables*, 40–41.
15. Ibid., 96–97. The discussion of these plot types of fiction literature is found in Frye, *Anatomy of Criticism*, 33–67.
16. See Via, *Parables*, 110–76. The tragic parables are: the Talents (Matt 25:14–30), the Ten Maidens (Matt 25:1–13), the Wedding Garment (Matt 22:11–14), the Wicked Tenants (Mark 12:1–9), and the Unforgiving Servant (Matt 18:23–35). The comic parables are the Workers in the Vineyard (Matt 20:1–16), the Unjust Steward (Luke 16:1–9), and the Prodigal Son (Luke 15:11–32).
17. Via, *Parables*, 96.
18. Holman and Harmon, *Handbook to Literature*, 400.
19. See Via, *Parables*, 147–55.
20. Via, *Parables*, 149.
21. Ibid., 148. Matthew's interpretation focuses on the fact that the workers in the parable are paid in reverse order.
22. Ibid.
23. Ibid., 150.
24. Ibid. Via does not adequately resolve the problem about whose story is being told in the parable, though he clearly takes the vineyard owner as the chief character. If the workers hired first were the protagonists, then the story would be tragic.
25. Ibid.
26. Ibid., 151.
27. Ibid.
28. Ibid., 100–101. Via draws these aspects of Greek tragedy from Aristotle.
29. Holman and Harmon, *Handbook to Literature*, 502.
30. Via, *Parables*, 151.
31. Ibid., 152.
32. Ibid.
33. Ibid., 153–54.

34. Ibid., 154.
35. Ibid., 155.
36. Ibid., 95.
37. Norman Perrin, "Biblical Scholarship in a New Vein," *Int* 21 (1967): 465–69. Virtually all reviewers of *The Parables* were positive: for example, William G. Doty, *JAAR* 36 (1968): 144–45; Wesley Kort, *ChrCent* 84 (1967): 753–54; Lucetta Mowry, *JBL* 87 (1968): 218–20.
38. Perrin, "Biblical Scholarship," 466.
39. Kort, review of Via, 753.
40. Perrin, *Language of the Kingdom*, 154.
41. Via is an occasional footnote in studies that incorporate neither his literary nor existential insights; see, for example, the most recent commentary on the parables: Hultgren, *Parables of Jesus*. The study that comes closest to Via's literary and existential approach is Breech, *Silence of Jesus*.
42. Perrin, *Language of the Kingdom*, 154.
43. Ibid., 154–55.
44. Mowry, review of Via, 218.
45. See chapter 8.
46. Via, *Parables*, 151.
47. Perrin, "Biblical Scholarship," 467; see also my criticism in this regard in *Parables as Poetic Fictions*, 80–81.
48. See Jeremias, *Parables of Jesus*, 115–229; and Herzog, *Parables as Subversive Speech*, 53–73. Even Via projects specific historical contexts for the parables, but does not use them in analyzing the parables. For example, he thinks that the parable of the Laborers in the Vineyard was "probably originally told with reference to Jesus' opponents in order to defend his association with sinners and to attack any legalistic merit doctrine" (*Parables*, 149). See the discussion in chapter 2.
49. Compare the discussion of Herzog in chapter 8. The nature parables are A Mustard Seed (Mark 4:31–32; Matt 13:31b–32; Luke 13:19; *Thom* 20), A Sprouting Seed (Mark 4:26–29; *Thom* 21d), the Ear of Grain (*Sec. Book Jas.* 12:22–27), the Date Palm Shoot (*Sec. Book Jas.* 7:22–28), and A Sower (Mark 4:3–8; Matt 13:3b–8; Luke 8:5–8a; *Thom* 9).
50. Via, *Parables*, 25.
51. Ibid., 39.
52. Perrin, *Language of the Kingdom*, 155.
53. See Hedrick, *Parables as Poetic Fictions*, 28–35.
54. See Hedrick, *Parables as Poetic Fictions*, 16–17, 254–58.
55. Hedrick, *Parables as Poetic Fictions*, 35.
56. Ibid., 31.
57. See Hedrick, "Prolegomena to Reading Parables."
58. Dodd, *Parables of the Kingdom*, 5. See Funk's discussion of the point in his *Language, Hermeneutic, and Word of God*, 133–36.
59. Robert W. Funk, "The Good Samaritan as Metaphor," in Funk, *Parables and Presence*, 34.
60. Amos N. Wilder, *Jesus' Parables and the War of Myths*, 89–90.
61. Hedrick, *Parables as Poetic Fictions*, 34–35.
62. Frank Kermode, *The Sense of an Ending: Studies in the Theory of Fiction* (London: Oxford University Press, 1967), 39.
63. See Hedrick, "Unfinished Story about a Fig Tree."

64. Hedrick, "Unfinished Story about a Fig Tree," 178–80.
65. Ibid., 182–83.
66. Ibid., 184–86.
67. Ibid., 186–88.
68. See Hedrick, "Unfinished Story about a Fig Tree," 188–92.
69. For a discussion of the poetics of parables, see Hedrick, *Parables as Poetic Fictions*, 57–72.
70. The quote is from Blomberg, "Poetic Fiction, Subversive Speech," 117. Blomberg's review is the most critical, due in part to the radically different assumptions Blomberg and I make about the tradition. His comments, however, deserve to be noted: Hedrick's study fails to overturn the "overwhelming consensus that Jesus did indeed use parables as illustrations of the Kingdom of God. Nor is it likely . . . that it was anyone other than Jesus who first linked parables and the kingdom together" (but now see Hedrick, "Parable and Kingdom"). Hedrick's "observations about parables without introductory frames prove equally misleading," since "virtually every one of these parables does have a *concluding* frame that uses referential language." (I reject all introductions and conclusions to the parables as the work of the early church and in any case thirteen of thirty-eight parables do not have a concluding interpretation—about 34 percent.) "Hedrick's virtually total non-use of the whole area of research into rabbinic parables is a massive lacuna in his work." (I do not use the rabbinic parables because the sources for the parables are two hundred years and more after the time of Jesus; they are also not the closest parallels.) For other, more positive, reviews of *Parables as Poetic Fictions*, see Richard S. Ascough, *RelSRev* 22, no. 2 (1996): 157; Alicia Batten, *TJT* 13, no. 2 (1997): 278–79; W. G. Morrice, *ExpTim* 106 (1994): 377; John M. Court, *JTS* 47, no. 1 (1996): 421; R. Doran, *CBQ* 58 (1996): 549–50; Jacques Guillet, *RSR* 84, no. 3 (1996): 433–35; A. J. Levoratti, "Las parábolès como ficcionas poéticas. Commentario de libros," *RevistB* 59 (1997): 45–61; Richard E. Strelan, *Lutheran Theological Journal* 30 (1996): 90–91; J. H. Hunter, *Neot* 30, no. 1 (1996): 220–21.
71. Amos N. Wilder, *The Bible and the Literary Critic* (Minneapolis: Fortress, 1991), 126. Wilder reviewed a paper I presented at the Society of Biblical Literature in 1987: "Parables and the Kingdom: The Vision of Jesus in Fiction and Faith," in *Society of Biblical Literature 1987 Seminar Papers: One Hundred Twenty-Third Annual Meeting, December 5–8, 1987, Boston, Massachusetts* (ed. Kent H. Richards; SBL Seminar Papers 26; Atlanta: Scholars Press, 1987), 368–93. This paper was later revised and incorporated into *Parables as Poetic Fictions.*
72. Wilder, *Bible and the Literary Critic*, 127.
73. Ibid., 128.
74. Ibid., 129.
75. Ibid., 130.
76. Ibid., 131.

Chapter Ten: How Does a Parable Resonate?

1. Wilder, *Jesus' Parables and the War of Myths*, 89–90.
2. Words such as "so," "just so," "so also" are conclusion-drawing words and always outside the story.
3. For a discussion of the textual variations in Matt 21:28–30, see pp. 44–46 in Metzger. The main ideas are accessible to English-only readers.
4. See chapters 2 and 6 for brief discussions of this parable.

5. See Hedrick, *When History and Faith Collide*, for an accessible, brief introduction to the issue of the modern quest for the "historical Jesus." An accessible introduction to the issues surrounding the originality of the various versions of the parables can be found in Funk et al., *Parables of Jesus*. Readers will need to look up each version in each gospel in which it appears. For the parable of the Lost Sheep, see p. 38, or look up each parable in Robert W. Funk, Roy W. Hoover, and the Jesus Seminar, *The Five Gospels: The Search for the Authentic Words of Jesus* (New York: Macmillan, 1993).
6. Irene Jacob and Walter Jacob, "Flora," *ABD*, 2:803–17. Another dictionary with extensive entries is George Arthur Buttrick, ed., *The Interpreter's Dictionary of the Bible: An Illustrated Encyclopedia* (4 vols.; New York: Abingdon, 1962), with a one-volume supplement, Keith Crim, ed. (Nashville: Abingdon, 1976).
7. For a list of publications on each of the parables up to 1979, see Warren Kissinger, *The Parables of Jesus: A History of Interpretation and Bibliography* (American Theological Library Association Bibliography Series 4; Metuchen, N.J.: Scarecrow Press, 1979). Bibliographies on parables from 1980 to the present can be found in recent commentaries of the parables and in the journal *New Testament Abstracts*. Two of the most recent commentaries, from different perspectives, are Scott, *Hear Then the Parable*, and Hultgren, *Parables of Jesus*.
8. These are the Mishnah and the Talmuds.
9. A beginner's New Testament introduction is Stephen L. Harris, *The New Testament: A Student's Introduction* (4th ed.; Boston: McGraw-Hill, 2002), 36–93. An advanced introduction is Helmut Koester, *Introduction to the New Testament*, vol. 1, *History, Culture, and Religion of the Hellenistic Age* (2d ed.; New York: Walter de Gruyter, 1995), 197–271, 371–91. The reader will also find helpful the source book by Everett Ferguson, *Backgrounds of Early Christianity* (2d ed.; Grand Rapids: Eerdmans, 1993), 373–546.
10. On this parable, see the discussion in Hedrick, *Parables as Poetic Fictions*, 142–63.
11. Actually there are two voices in 12:20. One is a narrator ("But God said to him . . .") who quotes God directly addressing the character in the story ("Fool, this night your soul is required of you"), though there is no evidence that the rich man in the story ever heard the voice. Had he heard God speaking to him, then Luke 12:20 would be a part of the story; since he does not, then Luke 12:20 is not a part of the rich farmer's story.
12. See Linnemann, *Jesus of the Parables*, 13. The other instance is Matt 25:2 ("wise and foolish maidens"). I take Luke 18:2 to be a positive statement by the narrator; see Hedrick, *Parables as Poetic Fictions*, 194–97. The other instances Linnemann cites are appropriate comments made by characters in the parable and do not reflect the narrator's judgment on the character. Luke 12:20 is somewhat complicated, since God is neither the narrator nor a character in the drama of the Rich Farmer.
13. Hedrick, *Parables as Poetic Fictions*, 148–51.
14. Ibid., 149.
15. On the nature of a farmstead, see Hedrick, *Parables as Poetic Fictions*, 146–48.
16. For the documentation, see Hedrick, *Parables as Poetic Fictions*, 162–63.
17. Hedrick, *Parables as Poetic Fictions*, 163.
18. Ibid., 159.
19. Ibid., 161.

Epilogue

1. Mary Ann Tolbert, *Perspectives on the Parables: An Approach to Multiple Interpretations* (Philadelphia: Fortress, 1979), 115–16.
2. Wilder, *Bible and Literary Critic*, 128.
3. Ibid.
4. Ibid., 129.
5. Ibid., 130.
6. Kermode, *Sense of an Ending*, 39.

Bibliography

Abrams, M. H. *A Glossary of Literary Terms*. 6th ed. Fort Worth: Harcourt Brace, 1993.

Ascough, Richard S. Review of C. W. Hedrick, *Parables as Poetic Fictions*. *Religious Studies Review* 22, no. 2 (1996): 157.

Attridge, Harold W., ed. *Nag Hammadi Codex I (The Jung Codex): Introductions, Texts, Translations, Indices*. Nag Hammadi Studies 22–23. Leiden: E. J. Brill, 1985.

Bailey, Kenneth E. *Poet and Peasant and Through Peasant Eyes*. 2 vols. in 1. Grand Rapids: Eerdmans, 1976.

Batten, Alicia. Review of C. W. Hedrick, *Parables as Poetic Fictions*. *Toronto Journal of Theology* 13, no. 2 (1997): 278–79.

Beavis, Mary Ann. "The Foolish Landowner (Luke 12:16b–20)." Pages 55–68 in Shillington, ed. *Jesus and His Parables*.

———. "Parable and Fable." *Catholic Biblical Quarterly* 52 (1990): 473–98.

Blomberg, Craig L. *Interpreting the Parables*. Downers Grove, Ill.: InterVarsity Press, 1990.

———. "Interpreting the Parables of Jesus: Where Are We and Where Do We Go from Here?" *Catholic Biblical Quarterly* 53 (1991): 50–78.

———. "The Parables of Jesus: Current Trends and Needs in Research." Pages 231–54 in *Studying the Historical Jesus: Evaluations of Current Research*. Edited by Bruce Chilton and Craig Evans. Leiden: E. J. Brill, 1994.

———. "Poetic Fictions, Subversive Speech, and Proportional Analogy in the Parables: Are We Making Any Progress in Parable Research?" *Horizons in Biblical Theology* 18, no. 1 (1996): 115–32.

———. Review of W. R. Herzog II, *Parables as Subversive Speech*. *Critical Review of Books in Religion* 8 (1995): 227–29.

Bornkamm, Günther. *Jesus of Nazareth*. Translated by Irene and Fraser Mcluskey with James M. Robinson. London: Hodder & Stoughton, 1960 (German original, 1956).

Boucher, Madeleine. *The Mysterious Parable: A Literary Study*. Catholic Biblical Quarterly Monograph Series 6. Washington, D.C.: The Catholic Biblical Association, 1977.

———. *The Parables*. Rev. ed. New Testament Message 7. Wilmington, Del.: Michael Glazier, 1983.

Breech, James. *The Silence of Jesus: The Authentic Voice of the Historical Man*. Philadelphia: Fortress, 1983.

Bruce, Alexander Balman. *The Parabolic Teaching of Christ: A Systematic and Critical Study of the Parables of Our Lord*. 3d rev. ed. New York: Armstrong & Son, 1886 (1st ed., 1882).

Bunyan, John. *The Pilgrim's Progress from This World to That Which Is to Come Delivered under the Similitude of a Dream: Wherein Is Discovered the Manner of His Setting Out, His Dangerous Journey and Safe Arrival at the Desired Country*. London: J. & J. Cundee, 1811.

Buttrick, George Arthur, ed. *The Interpreter's Dictionary of the Bible: An Illustrated Encyclopedia*. 4 vols. New York: Abingdon, 1962.

Butts, James R. "The Progymnasmata of Theon: A New Text with Translation and Commentary." Ph.D. diss., Claremont Graduate School, 1986.

Cameron, Ron. *Sayings Traditions in the Apocryphon of James*. Harvard Theological Studies 34. Philadelphia: Fortress, 1984.

Carlston, Charles E. *The Parables of the Triple Tradition*. Philadelphia: Fortress, 1975.

Ciardi, John. *How Does a Poem Mean?* Part 3 of *An Introduction to Literature*. Boston: Houghton Mifflin, 1959.

Court, John M. Review of C. W. Hedrick, *Parables as Poetic Fictions*. *Journal of Theological Studies* 47, no. 1 (1996): 421.

Crim, Keith, ed. *The Interpreter's Dictionary of the Bible: An Illustrated Encyclopedia*. Supplementary Volume. Nashville: Abingdon, 1976.

Crossan, John Dominic. *In Fragments: The Aphorisms of Jesus*. San Francisco: Harper & Row, 1983.

———. *In Parables: The Challenge of the Historical Jesus*. New York: Harper & Row, 1973.

———. "Parable." Pages 146–52 in Freedman, ed., *Anchor Bible Dictionary*, vol. 5.

———. Review of W. R. Herzog II, *Parables as Subversive Speech*. *Biblical Theology Bulletin* 25, no. 3 (1995): 145.

———. *Sayings Parallels: A Workbook for the Jesus Tradition*. Foundations and Facets. Philadelphia: Fortress, 1986.

Davies, Stevan. *The Gospel of Thomas Annotated and Explained*. Woodstock, Vt.: Skylight Paths, 2002.

Dodd, C. H. *The Parables of the Kingdom*. New York: Charles Scribner's Sons, 1936.

Donahue, John R. *The Gospel in Parable: Metaphor, Narrative, and Theology in the Synoptic Gospels*. Philadelphia: Fortress, 1988.

Doran, Robert. Review of C. W. Hedrick, *Parables as Poetic Fictions*. *Catholic Biblical Quarterly* 58 (1996): 549–50.

Doty, William G. Review of D. O. Via Jr., *The Parables*. *Journal of the American Academy of Religion* 36 (1968): 144–45.

Downing, F. Gerald. Review of W. R. Herzog II, *Parables as Subversive Speech*. *Theology* 98 (1995): 386–87.

Ferguson, Everett. *Backgrounds of Early Christianity*. 2d ed. Grand Rapids: Eerdmans, 1993.

Fiebig, Paul. *Die Gleichnisreden Jesu im Lichte der rabbinischen Gleichnisse des neutestamentlichen Zeitalters*. Tübingen: J. C. B. Mohr (Paul Siebeck), 1912.

Ford, Richard Q. *The Parables of Jesus: Recovering the Art of Listening*. Minneapolis: Fortress, 1997.

Francis, Robert. "The Hound." Page 62 in Perrine, *Sound and Sense*.
Freedman, David Noel, ed. *The Anchor Bible Dictionary*. 6 vols. New York: Doubleday, 1992.
Freese, John Henry. *Aristotle: The "Art" of Rhetoric*. Cambridge, Mass.: Harvard University Press, 1947.
Frost, Robert. "Bereft." Page 62 in Perrine, *Sound and Sense*.
Frye, Northrop. *Anatomy of Criticism: Four Essays*. Princeton, N.J.: Princeton University Press, 1957.
Funk, Robert W. "The Good Samaritan as Metaphor." Pages 29–34 in Funk, *Parables and Presence*.
———. "How Do You Read? (Luke 10:25–37)." *Interpretation* 18 (1964): 56–61.
———. *Language, Hermeneutic, and Word of God*. New York: Harper & Row, 1966.
———. *Parables and Presence: Forms of the New Testament Tradition*. Philadelphia: Fortress, 1982.
Funk, Robert W., Roy W. Hoover, and the Jesus Seminar. *The Five Gospels: The Search for the Authentic Words of Jesus*. New York: Macmillan, 1993.
Funk, Robert W., Bernard Brandon Scott, and James R. Butts. *The Parables of Jesus: Red Letter Edition. A Report of the Jesus Seminar*. Sonoma, Calif.: Polebridge, 1988.
Fyfe, W. Hamilton and W. Rhys Roberts. *Aristotle, The Poetics; "Longinus," On the Sublime; Demetrius, On Style*. Cambridge, Mass.: Harvard University Press, 1953.
Guerin, Wilfred L., Earle Labor, Lee Morgan, Jeanne C. Reesman, and John R. Willingham. *A Handbook of Critical Approaches to Literature*. 3d. ed. New York: Oxford University Press, 1992.
Guillet, Jacques. Review of C. W. Hedrick, *Parables as Poetic Fictions*. *Recherches de science religieuse* 84, no. 3 (1996): 433–35.
Harmon, A. M. *Lucian with an English Translation*. 8 vols. New York: Macmillan, 1913.
Harris, Stephen L. *The New Testament: A Student's Introduction*. 4th ed. Boston: McGraw-Hill, 2002.
Hazo, Samuel. "Affective Fallacy." Page 8 in Preminger et al., eds., *Princeton Encyclopedia of Poetry*.
Hedrick, Charles W. "An Anecdotal Argument for the Independence of the *Gospel of Thomas* from the Synoptic Gospels." Pages 113–26 in *For the Children, Perfect Instruction: Studies in Honor of Hans-Martin Schenke on the Occasion of the Berliner Arbeitskreis für koptisch-gnostische Schriften's Thirtieth Year*. Edited by Hans-Gephard Bethge, Stephen Emmel, Karen L. King, and Imke Schletterer. Leiden: E. J. Brill, 2002.
———. "The Gospel of Thomas and Early Christian Tradition." In *Varia Gnostica*. Edited by Marianne Aagaard Skovmand, Søren Giversen, and Jesper Hyldahl. Copenhagen: The Royal Danish Society of Sciences, Historical-Philosophical Information, forthcoming.
———. "Kingdom Sayings and Parables of Jesus in the *Apocryphon of James*: Tradition and Redaction." *New Testament Studies* 29, no. 1 (1983): 1–24.
———. "The Lion's Tooth," *Shiftless Stone Review* 1 (1991): 2.
———. "Parable and Kingdom: A Survey of the Evidence in Mark." *Perspectives in Religious Studies* 27, no. 2 (Summer 2000): 179–99.
———. "Parables and the Kingdom: The Vision of Jesus in Fiction and Faith." Pages 362–93 in Richards, ed., *Society of Biblical Literature 1987 Seminar Papers*.
———. *Parables as Poetic Fictions: The Creative Voice of Jesus*. Peabody, Mass.: Hendrickson, 1994.

———. "Prolegomena to Reading Parables: Luke 13:6–9 as a Test Case." *Review and Expositer* 94, no. 2 (1997): 179–97.

———. "The Thirty-Four Gospels." *Bible Review* 18, no. 3 (2000): 20–31, 46–47.

———. "An Unfinished Story about a Fig Tree in a Vineyard (Luke 13:6–9)." *Perspectives in Religious Studies* 26, no. 2 (Summer 1999): 169–92.

———. *When History and Faith Collide: Studying Jesus*. Peabody, Mass.: Hendrickson, 1999.

Hengel, Martin. *Judaism and Hellenism: Studies in Their Encounter in Palestine during the Early Hellenistic Period*. 2 vols. in 1. Translated by John Bowden. Philadelphia: Fortress, 1974.

Herzog, William R. II. *Parables as Subversive Speech: Jesus as Pedagogue of the Oppressed*. Louisville, Ky.: Westminster John Knox, 1994.

Holman, C. Hugh, and William Harmon. *A Handbook to Literature*. 5th ed. New York: Macmillan, 1986.

Hoover, Roy W., ed. *Profiles of Jesus*. Santa Rosa, Calif.: Polebridge, 2002.

Howatson, M. C. *The Oxford Companion to Classical Literature*. 2d ed. New York: Oxford University Press, 1989.

Hultgren, Arland J. *The Parables of Jesus: A Commentary*. Grand Rapids: Eerdmans, 2000.

Hunter, J. H. Review of C. W. Hedrick, *Parables as Poetic Fictions*. *Neotestamentica* 30, no. 1 (1996): 220–21.

Hurtik, Emil, and Robert Yarber. *An Introduction to Poetry and Criticism*. Lexington, Mass.: Xerox College Publishing, 1972.

Iser, Wolfgang. *The Act of Reading: A Theory of Aesthetic Response*. Baltimore: Johns Hopkins University Press, 1978.

Jacob, Irene, and Walter Jacob. "Flora." Pages 803–17 in Freedman, ed., *Anchor Bible Dictionary*, vol. 2.

Jeremias, Joachim. *The Parables of Jesus*. Translated by S. H. Hooke (from the German 6th ed., 1962). Rev. ed. New York: Charles Scribner's Sons, 1963.

Johnson, Luke Timothy. Review of W. R. Herzog II, *Parables as Subversive Speech*. *Theological Studies* 56, no. 3 (1995): 571–72.

Jones, Peter Rhea. *Studying the Parables of Jesus*. Macon, Ga.: Smyth & Helwys, 1999.

———. *The Teaching of the Parables*. Nashville: Broadman, 1982.

Jülicher, Adolf. *Die Gleichnisreden Jesu*. 2 vols. Leipzig: J. C. B. Mohr (Paul Siebeck), 1899.

Keesey, Donald, ed. *Contexts for Criticism*. 3d ed. Mountain View, Calif.: Mayfield, 1998.

Kennedy, X. J. *An Introduction to Poetry*. Boston: Little, Brown & Co., 1966.

Kermode, Frank. *The Sense of an Ending: Studies in the Theory of Fiction*. London: Oxford University Press, 1967.

Kissinger, Warren. *The Parables of Jesus: A History of Interpretation and Bibliography*. American Theological Library Association Bibliography Series 4. Metuchen, N.J.: Scarecrow Press, 1979.

Koester, Helmut. *Introduction to the New Testament*. Vol. 1, *History, Culture, and Religion of the Hellenistic Age*. 2d ed. New York: Walter de Gruyter, 1995.

———. "The Text of the Synoptic Gospels in the Second Century." Pages 19–37. *Gospel Traditions in the Second Century: Origins, Recensions, Text, and Transmission*. Edited by William L. Petersen. Notre Dame, Ind.: University of Notre Dame Press, 1989.

Kort, Wesley. Review of D. O. Via Jr., *The Parables*. *Christian Century* 84 (1967): 753–54.

Kümmel, Werner Georg. *Introduction to the New Testament*. Translated by Howard C. Kee. 17th ed. Nashville: Abingdon, 1975.

Lane, William L. *The Gospel according to Mark*. The New International Commentary on the New Testament 2. Grand Rapids: Eerdmans, 1974.

Levoratti, A. J. "Las parábolas como ficcionas poéticas. Comentario de libros." *Revista Biblica* 59 (1997): 45–61.

Linnemann, Eta. *Jesus of the Parables: Introduction and Exposition*. Translated by John Sturdy. New York: Harper & Row, 1966.

Main, C. F., and Peter J. Seng. *Poems*. 2d ed. Belmont, Calif.: Wadsworth, 1965.

Martin, Dale B. "Social-Scientific Criticism." Pages 125–41 in *To Each Its Own Meaning: An Introduction to Biblical Criticisms and Their Application*. Edited by Steven L. McKenzie and Stephen R. Haynes. Rev. and expanded ed. Louisville, Ky.: Westminster John Knox, 1999.

Matthews, Victor H., and Don C. Benjamin, eds. *Old Testament Parallels: Laws and Stories from the Ancient Near East*. Rev. and expanded ed. New York: Paulist Press, 1997.

Metzger, Bruce M. *A Textual Commentary on the Greek New Testament*. 2d ed. New York: United Bible Societies, 1994.

Miller, Robert J., ed. *The Complete Gospels: Annotated Scholars Version*. Rev. and expanded ed. Sonoma, Calif.: Polebridge, 1992.

Morrice, W. G. Review of C. W. Hedrick, *Parables as Poetic Fictions*. *Expository Times* 106 (1994): 377.

Mowry, Lucetta. Review of D. O. Via Jr., *The Parables*. *Journal of Biblical Literature* 87 (1968): 218–20.

Nestle, Eberhard, Erwin Nestle, Barbara Aland, and Kurt Aland. *Greek-English New Testament*. Stuttgart: Deutsche Bibelgesellshaft, 1998.

Oesterley, W. O. E. *The Gospel Parables in the Light of Their Jewish Background*. London: S.P.C.K., 1936.

Parsons, Mikeal C. "'Allegorizing Allegory': Narrative Analysis and Parable Interpretation." *Perspectives in Religious Studies* 15, no. 2 (1988): 147–64.

———. "The Critical Use of the Rabbinic Literature in New Testament Studies." *Perspectives in Religious Studies* 12 (Summer 1985): 85–102.

Perrin, Norman. *Jesus and the Language of the Kingdom: Symbol and Metaphor in New Testament Interpretation*. Philadelphia: Fortress, 1976.

———. "Biblical Scholarship in a New Vein" (review of Dan Otto Via Jr., *The Parables*). *Interpretation* 21 (1967): 465–69.

Perrine, Laurence. *Sound and Sense: An Introduction to Poetry*. 5th ed. New York: Harcourt Brace Jovanovich, 1977.

Perry, Ben Edward. *Aesopica: A Series of Texts relating to Aesop or Ascribed to Him or Closely Connected with the Literary Tradition That Bears His Name. Collected and Critically Edited, in Part Translated from Oriental Languages with a Commentary and Historical Essay*. Vol. 1, *Greek and Latin Texts*. Urbana, Ill.: University of Illinois, 1952.

———. *Babrius and Phaedrus: Newly Edited and Translated into English, together with an Historical Introduction and a Comprehensive Survey of Greek and Latin Fables in the Aesopic Tradition*. Cambridge, Mass.: Harvard University Press, 1984.

Preminger, Alex, Frank J. Warnke, and O. B. Hardison, Jr., eds. *Princeton Encyclopedia of Poetry and Poetics*. Enlarged ed. Princeton, N.J.: Princeton University Press, 1974.

Priest, Paul. Review of W. R. Herzog II, *Parables as Subversive Speech*. *Horizons in Biblical Theology* 18, no. 1 (1996): 110–11.

Reid, Barbara E. Review of W. R. Herzog II, *Parables as Subversive Speech*. *Catholic Biblical Quarterly* 58 (1996): 348–49.

Richards, Kent H., ed. *Society of Biblical Literature 1987 Seminar Papers: One Hundred Twenty-Third Annual Meeting, December 5–8, 1987, Boston, Massachusetts*. Society of Biblical Literature Seminar Papers 26. Atlanta: Scholars Press, 1987.

Roberts, C. H. *An Unpublished Fragment of the Fourth Gospel in the John Rylands Library*. Manchester: John Rylands Library, 1935.

Robinson, James M. "Jesus' Parables as God Happening." Pages 45–52 in *A Meeting of Poets and Theologians to Discuss Parable, Myth, and Language*. Edited by Tony Stoneburner. Cambridge, Mass.: Church Society for College Work, 1968.

———., ed. *The Nag Hammadi Library in English*. 3d completely rev. ed. San Francisco: Harper & Row, 1988.

Rohrbaugh, Richard L. "A Dysfunctional Family and Its Neighbors (Luke 15:11b–32)." Pages 141–64 in Shillington, ed., *Jesus and His Parables*.

Sanday, William. *The Gospels in the Second Century: An Examination of the Critical Part of a Work Entitled "Supernatural Religion."* London: Macmillan, 1876.

Sanders, E. P., and Margaret Davies. *Studying the Synoptic Gospels*. Philadelphia: Trinity Press International, 1989.

Schiffman, Lawrence H. *From Text to Tradition: A History of Second Temple Judaism*. Hoboken, N.J.: KTAV Publishing House, 1991.

Scott, Bernard Brandon. *Hear Then the Parable: A Commentary on the Parables of Jesus*. Minneapolis: Fortress, 1989.

Shillington, V. George, ed. *Jesus and His Parables: Interpreting the Parables of Jesus Today*. Edinburgh: T. & T. Clark, 1997.

Stallman, R. W. "Intentions, problem of." Pages 398–400 in Preminger et al., eds., *Princeton Encyclopedia of Poetry*.

Stein, Robert H. *An Introduction to the Parables of Jesus*. Philadelphia: Westminster, 1981.

Steinmann, Martin Jr. "Heresy of Paraphrase." Pages 344–45 in Preminger et al., eds., *Princeton Encyclopedia of Poetry*.

Sternberg, Meier. *Expositional Modes and Temporal Ordering in Fiction*. Baltimore: Johns Hopkins University Press, 1978.

———. *The Poetics of Biblical Narrative: Ideological Literature and the Drama of Reading*. Bloomington, Ind.: Indiana University Press, 1987.

Stevens, Wallace. *Letters of Wallace Stevens*. Edited by Holly Stevens. New York: Alfred A. Knopf, 1966.

Strelan, Richard E. Review of C. W. Hedrick, *Parables as Poetic Fictions*. *Lutheran Theological Journal* 30 (1996): 90–91.

Taylor, Vincent. *The Gospel according to St. Mark*. New York: Macmillan, 1959.

Thackery, H. St. J., ed. and trans. *Josephus: The Jewish War*. 8 vols. New York: Putnam, 1928.

Tolbert, Mary Ann. *Perspectives on the Parables: An Approach to Multiple Interpretations*. Philadelphia: Fortress, 1979.

Trench, Richard C. *Notes on the Parables of Our Lord*. London: Pickering & Inglis, 1953 (1st ed., 1841).

Via, Dan Otto Jr. *The Parables: Their Literary and Existential Dimension*. Philadelphia: Fortress, 1967.

Wenham, David. *The Parables of Jesus*. Downers Grove, Ill.: InterVarsity, 1989.

Wilder, Amos N. *The Bible and the Literary Critic*. Minneapolis: Fortress, 1991.

———. *Early Christian Rhetoric: The Language of the Gospel.* Peabody, Mass.: Hendrickson, 1999 (1st ed., 1964).

———. *Jesus' Parables and the War of Myths: Essays on Imagination in the Scriptures.* Edited by James Breech. Philadelphia: Fortress, 1982.

———. *The Language of the Gospel: Early Christian Rhetoric.* New York: Harper & Row, 1964.

Wimsatt, W. K. Jr., and M. C. Beardsley. "The Intentional Fallacy." *Sewanee Review* 54 (1946): 468–88.

Young, Brad H. *The Parables: Jewish Tradition and Christian Interpretation.* Peabody, Mass.: Hendrickson, 1998.

Index of Ancient Sources

Early Christian and Related Literature

Index of Modern Authors

Index of Parable Titles

None of the stories of Jesus known from the New Testament gospels and other early Christian literature are given titles in ancient texts. A list of ancient parable titles, however, is found in the *Secret Book of James* (8:1–10), but whether these titles correspond to the actual stories known from other sources is uncertain. More or less customary titles for the existing stories have evolved in Christian tradition, however. These customary titles to the story are usually based on a religious interpretation of the story or on the basis of value judgments on the behavior of the assumed principal characters in the stories. The customary titles telescope the meaning of a traditional reading of the story. To avoid this prejudicing of the story for the reader, Brandon Scott has proposed a new way of titling the stories (*Hear Then the Parable*, 460) by identifying them, for the most part, on the basis of their *incipits* (that is, their first lines), which was the way ancient documents, lacking a prescript or postscript title, would have been titled in antiquity. In this book, parables are titled, more or less, using the customary titles in order to facilitate an easier identification of the story by the reader. All titles used for a given story are listed below.

Index of Selected Terms Related to Parables